# Navigating Law School's Waters:
# A Guide to Success

This book is dedicated

To my parents, Gemma and Patrick Grande, who taught me how to write.

To my husband, Jon Montana, who encourages me to keep writing.

And to my children, Jonathan, Ryan and Michael, who I now teach how to write.

# Navigating Law School's Waters:
# A Guide to Success

Patricia Grande Montana

VANDEPLAS PUBLISHING LLC

UNITED STATES OF AMERICA

Navigating Law School's Waters: A Guide to Success

Montana, Patricia Grande

Published by:

Vandeplas Publishing LLC – February 2014

801 International Parkway, 5th Floor
Lake Mary, FL. 32746
USA

www.vandeplaspublishing.com

ISBN 978-1-60042-163-1

# TABLE OF CONTENTS

# Introduction

Law school, particularly the first year, can be a rather intimidating and challenging experience for many students. As a law student, you are expected to read hundreds of pages of judicial opinions and other legal authorities a week. In addition to the large volume of reading, the reading itself is dense. It contains legal jargon and many new terms of art as well as rules of procedure and citation that, at least initially, will be foreign to you. You are also expected to prepare notes on what you have read so that you can follow class lectures and respond intelligently to your professors' Socratic questioning, which oftentimes can seem vague and unpredictable. Finally, you are expected to demonstrate your knowledge of the law usually on a single, closed-book exam at the end of the semester. For the most part, that exam is your one chance to do well in a course, as effort and class participation typically have little or no influence on final grades.

These expectations, and particularly the pressures surrounding final exams, present significant challenges for all students—whether they have come directly from an undergraduate or another post-graduate program or have previously worked in the legal field or another profession altogether. Despite these challenges, whatever your background, you will be happy to know that law school is an entirely navigable body of water. Thus, there is no need for any student to drown, or even feel like they are drowning, in the law school experience. All you need are the proper tools to successfully navigate your way through it. The purpose of this book is to give you those tools as well as meaningful opportunities to practice using them. The goal is for you to be able to sail smoothly through the experience with great skill and confidence.

Though you will find similar guidance in other first-year introduction to law school texts, this book is unique in that it takes a cognitive approach to its instruction. It is premised on the belief that students learn new information best when they have a "schema" or framework that allows them to think logically about the information. We build schemata from past experiences. As we receive new information, we give it meaning based on how it fits into our pre-existing schemata. As we refine our understanding of the new information, we identify connections between concepts, enabling us to expand or modify existing schemata as well as create new ones.

Without experience in the law, law students often have no pre-existing schemata for the type of reading, analysis, and writing that law school requires. This book helps students meet the demands of law school by giving them the appropriate schemata so that they can more easily make sense of the new information. To that end, this book routinely draws on non-legal examples when introducing new topics and skills, and spends substantial time explaining why law students are instructed to read and brief cases, outline, study, and write exam answers the way they are. Also, this book often builds upon the same core legal problems throughout the text, including in the exercises, so that students can more easily master the relevant skills. With this context, law students are able to draw analogies between their past experiences and the new information in a logical and manageable way, allowing them to fit the new information into a new schema. Thus, this book provides more than just written instructions on how to navigate law school's waters; it shows law students how to do so, thereby making them captains of their own success.

That success is dependent first on an understanding of what law school is intended to teach. You have likely heard that law school trains students to think like lawyers. That is true. But, what does the expression "thinking like a lawyer" really mean? In short, it means having the ability to analyze and solve legal problems. The skills courses you take in law school, starting with your legal analysis and writing class in the first semester of your first year, explicitly teach you how to analyze and solve legal problems. They present a mix of real and hypothetical questions that you must research and answer. You are then expected to communicate your analysis and your support for it in some type of predictive or persuasive writing or oral presentation.

Your doctrinal courses likewise teach you how to problem solve, though with usually fewer opportunities outside of the final exam to practice doing it. Instead, these courses examine in depth the law of a specific subject area. You might be surprised to learn, however, that simply knowing the law and recalling it at exam time is usually not enough to excel in these types of courses. Your professors want to know that you are also capable of appropriately applying your knowledge of the law to a new fact scenario. Ultimately, that is what you are tested on—your ability to solve a hypothetical exam problem and explain your basis. Because this process, referred to as legal analysis or legal reasoning, is so important to your success in all of your law school classes, skills and doctrinal ones alike, this book introduces you to it as early as Chapter 1. It is crucial that you know upfront how your reading and briefing of cases, outlining, studying, legal writing, and law school exams are all geared toward teaching legal analysis—the main ingredient for "thinking like a lawyer".

Chapter 1 is titled *Understanding Legal Analysis* to remind you that your journey through law school centers on understanding legal analysis. The foundational skills of how to read cases as well as brief cases and take effective class notes are all relevant to your understanding of legal analysis and discussed in Chapters 2 and 3, respectively. These chapters have inter-related, hands-on exercises to ensure that you master the skills before applying them to real legal problems. Chapter 4, on outlining, is an important chapter and one that is not usually covered in introduction to law school books with the same level of depth as is here. Though there is substantial literature on how to create outlines and analyze legal problems, there is virtually no discussion on the relationship between the two—that is, how to use an outline to analyze and answer a legal question. Chapter 4 provides that essential discussion. Chapter 5 brings it all together and teaches you how to use what you have learned to analyze real legal problems.

However, your ability to analyze legal problems will go unnoticed in both law school and practice if you are unable to effectively communicate your analysis in writing. Chapter 6 thus addresses this topic in great detail. As you have probably guessed, the most prevalent form of writing in law school is writing for an exam. Among other things, this chapter discusses how writing an exam answer is analogous to the type of writing covered in most first-year legal writing courses. It can be predictive writing—writing that predicts the likely outcome of a legal problem. Or, it can be persuasive writing—writing that argues that a certain outcome is the right one. Using the analytical framework of IRAC (an acronym for Issue, Rule,

Application, and Conclusion—the main components of a written legal analysis), this chapter explains these connections and describes with specificity how to write a model exam answer.

Related to exam writing, the next chapter, Chapter 7, offers some practical suggestions on how to sail through the studying and taking of exams. It tackles topics, such as time management, study groups, and practice exams. Because students vary in their learning styles, it also offers several different approaches to these topics. Finally, no introduction to law school text would be complete or helpful without a discussion of your emotional and psychological well-being while in law school. Without question, there will be moments when the pressure of the experience will seem overwhelming. To manage that pressure, you will need to maintain a positive attitude and keep a healthy mind and body. Thus, this book's final chapter, Chapter 8, addresses the importance of caring for these areas.

In the end, this book should give you all that you need to navigate law school's waters. You should follow the order of the book, re-read chapters when necessary, and master the accompanying exercises before moving forward, as each chapter intentionally builds on the previous one. With this book as your guide, law school success is completely attainable. If you simply stay focused on your destination and work diligently to get there, you can achieve that success. Enjoy your journey!

# Acknowledgements

I would like to thank St. John's University School of Law and my Dean, Michael A. Simons, for fully supporting my work on this book. I would also like to thank my students for motivating me to put to paper what I have been teaching for many years now.

I owe the most thanks to my husband, though. Without his boundless support and encouragement, projects like this one would never be possible. He is my inspiration. Thank you.

# — Chapter 1 —

# Understanding Legal Analysis

Legal analysis is the process lawyers use to predict how a court will likely resolve a legal question. That process, as you will soon discover, is highly structured and therefore best explained using a straightforward example. Suppose a friend asks you, now a lawyer who was recently admitted to the bar, whether she is required to leash her dogs when walking them on the town's public streets and sidewalks. The question is uncomplicated, but nonetheless requires some research before you can answer it. As the first step, you check to see whether your town has a leash law. Let's assume that you locate an ordinance that expressly states that dogs must be leashed at all times while on public property. Your friend's question thus has a definitive answer. She must leash her dogs at all times while walking them on the town's public streets and sidewalks. This answer is also your prediction for how a court would rule if ever presented with the same legal question. In reaching this prediction, you engaged in legal analysis in its simplest form.

This is the same process lawyers follow when the questions become more complex or involved. Therefore, let's review what the basic steps to legal analysis are using the simple example above before advancing on to more difficult ones. First, we isolated the legal issue we needed to research (i.e., whether a dog must be leashed when on town public property).

### Basic Steps to Legal Analysis

1. *Isolate legal issues*
2. *Research relevant law*
3. *Apply law to fact scenario*
4. *Resolve issues*

This step was almost automatic because there were so few facts to consider and the question was very specific. Next, we researched the relevant law. The law—the ordinance's plain language—was an unambiguous rule that squarely resolved the legal issue. Finally, we applied that law to the factual question, thereby reaching an answer. These are the basic steps to legal analysis. Because the factual question we were analyzing was completely addressed by the language of the law itself, the answer was clear. In law school, we refer to these types of issues as undisputed ones because they are so easily resolved by a legal rule. There is no argument that your friend does not have to leash her dogs. In other words, no one would dispute the way in which you analyzed the legal issue.

Now let's look at a more complicated question on the same topic. This question raises a disputed issue—one that is not so easily answered by the law—as well as several undisputed ones. The problem is as follows:

> Your client, Michael Gerardi, was walking his unleashed dog, a Golden Retriever, in a public park when the dog bit a young boy, causing injuries to the boy's leg. The boy was playing on the sidewalk, unaware of the dog, until the bite. The boy sought medical attention from a local hospital's emergency room. His parents have sent Mr. Gerardi the hospital bill along with a demand for reimbursement. Your client would like to know whether he is obligated to pay the bill.
>
> According to your client, his dog is gentle; however, there was one prior incident in which the dog scratched a stranger. The dog was similarly unleashed at the time. However, the stranger required no medical attention.

To begin, we must isolate the legal issues. Unlike in the earlier example, the client's question here is broader than the legal question we must research. The client wants to know whether he must pay the child's medical expenses. This is typical of the types of questions clients will ask. They are interested in the bottom line, knowing whether they will win or lose, not the specific legal issues that inform that bottom line. Nonetheless, you must start your analysis by defining the legal issues, as your predictions on how a court will likely resolve them is the only way to reach the bottom line answer.

Thus, the legal question must be narrowly tailored to the problem first. This is another way of saying that the question must be fact-specific, not general or vague. For Mr. Gerardi's question, the most important facts are (1) he walked his dog without a leash; (2) he was in a public park; (3) the child did not provoke the dog; (4) the child was injured; and (5) the dog had previously scratched another person when unleashed.

We must now pull together these facts to formulate a narrower legal question than the one Mr. Gerardi originally asked. In doing so, the question becomes whether a dog owner is responsible for injuries caused to another by his dog where that dog was unprovoked and in a public park without a leash and had previously injured another person when unleashed. If the question were not this specific, your research would be unfocused. For example, a question that simply asked whether a dog owner is liable for injuries caused by his dog would require you to research all the scenarios in which that owner is responsible—a task that would be both timely and costly. That question omits the dog's prior history as well as the fact that the dog was unleashed, unprovoked, and on public property, facts which are critical in determining your client's liability.

After framing the legal question, the next step to analyzing this problem is to research the relevant law. Let's imagine that after some preliminary research, you discover that your state has a statute that reads as follows:

**IT IS UNLAWFUL FOR AN OWNER TO PERMIT A DANGEROUS DOG TO GO BEYOND THE OWNER'S REAL PROPERTY UNLESS THE DOG IS LEASHED AND MUZZLED**[1]

Before we continue researching the relevant law, the language of this statute demands that we divide the legal question into several subparts. These subparts will become the legal issues we will need to analyze later. Whenever examining statutory language or any rules for that matter, it is useful to separate the elements in some numerical fashion. The goal is to rewrite the language of the statute in a more understandable and usable form. In this example, it is easiest to think of the conditions that must exist to establish a dog owner's liability. An owner will be liable only if: (1) the dog is dangerous; (2) the dog is not on the owner's real property; and (3) the dog is either unleashed or unmuzzled or both. These three elements are the

---

[1] This is a fictitious statute; yet, it is inspired by North Carolina's current state law on the topic.

three issues that need to be resolved. The third element requires an "or" clause because a dangerous dog must be both leashed and muzzled in order to avoid liability. In matching the elements of this statute to the client's facts, we quickly see that two of the issues (elements 2 and 3) are undisputed. The dog was in a public park, not on his private property, and the dog was not wearing a leash or muzzle. Like the first example in this chapter, we quickly moved through the steps to legal analysis with respect to these two issues because the facts were squarely addressed by the language of the statute itself.

*Steps to Legal Analysis with Greater Detail*

1. *Isolate legal issues*
   a. *Identify undisputed issues*
   b. *Identify disputed issues*
2. *Research relevant law*
   a. *Read cases*
   b. *Synthesize legal rule*
3. *Apply rule to fact scenario*
4. *Resolve legal issues*

However, the first element—whether the dog is dangerous—is disputed because the statute itself does not explain what the word "dangerous" means. Though the word alone is not ambiguous, the word as applied to the problem creates ambiguity. It is unclear whether a dog that injured a young child without provocation is "dangerous" when that dog is generally gentle, but scratched another stranger in the past. That is the disputed issue we must resolve next. Though you might have a personal opinion as to whether the dog is dangerous, it frankly does not matter. What matters is what the law says about the word "dangerous". This requires that we spend more time researching how courts interpret that language. Thus, the steps to analyzing disputed legal issues like this one are necessarily more involved and, as a result, more time consuming, than the steps to analyzing undisputed issues.

To review where we are in the process, which is depicted with more detail above, we have just reached the second step. For that step, our goal is to research the relevant law and find the legal rule that applies to the disputed issue of dangerousness.

# A Quick Detour. . . What is a legal rule?

For first-year students, there is much anxiety over finding the correct legal rule and presenting it accurately. That anxiety usually stems from a misconception that the rule must be articulated in a single sentence or in some formulaic way. Simply

*A legal rule is a statement of the law that controls how an issue should be resolved.*

stated, a legal rule is a statement of the law that controls how an issue should be resolved. It might set out conditions that must exist to achieve a specific result or list factors or interests that courts must weigh in resolving an issue. Oftentimes, it takes more than a single sentence to present a legal rule clearly and completely, particularly when it involves some sort of balancing test.

Sometimes legal rules are expressly stated in a statute or the case law. For example, returning to Mr. Gerardi's problem for a moment, if the statute itself or a case interpreting it explicitly defined the term "dangerous dog" as a dog that has previously injured (including scratched) a person when unprovoked, the legal rule would be that definition. Students usually do not have difficulty finding and stating such an explicit rule of law. However, many legal rules are not expressly stated. In these situations, the legal rule must be synthesized from the holdings of cases that address the same problem as yours. Rule synthesis, as law professors refer to this process, requires careful attention to what courts have said and done when faced with a similar set of facts. This task—encompassed in Step 2—is the one that students find the most difficult and thus merits the detailed explanation on synthesis that follows.

## Synthesizing Legal Rules

In the absence of an explicitly stated rule, you will need to read the relevant case law to figure out how courts typically resolve the disputed issue. Essentially what you will be looking for is the "formula" or "recipe" the courts follow when making their decisions. After reading several cases, you should begin to see a pattern in how courts approach the issue and reason through their decisions. You might notice that some facts are essential to reaching a particular decision, while others might be helpful, but are ultimately unnecessary. You might also notice that facts might be weighted differently. Whatever the case, once you are able to articulate the pattern (or stated differently, write down the recipe), you have synthesized the legal rule.

For Mr. Gerardi's problem, we need to find the legal rule for the word "dangerous." In other words, we need to know what courts consider in deciding whether a dog is dangerous. To get there, we will have to read all of the relevant case law interpreting that particular language of the statute. The pattern or recipe should become apparent after grouping the cases by their holdings—those that held dogs were dangerous and those that did not—and examining what was similar in the cases with like holdings and how they differed from the other cases. The facts of the cases together with the courts' reasoning for their decisions are what we will use to make sense of the similarities and differences in the holdings and ultimately to build a synthesized rule.

Because rule synthesis in the abstract is a difficult concept, it is worth looking at a non-legal illustration before returning to Mr. Gerardi's legal problem. Suppose a four-year-old would like to know whether his mother will let him have ice cream as a treat. He remembers having ice cream at birthday parties, the zoo, and the amusement park. He also remembers his mother giving him ice cream only after he finished all of his food, but not beforehand. There were other times when he wanted ice cream, but did not get it, like when he was fighting with his brother, throwing tantrums, or refusing to clean up his toys. If you were asked to explain to that four-year-old the circumstances under which his mother will give him ice cream, what would you say? You could certainly list the exact prior experiences that led to ice cream and those that did not; however, his current situation might not replicate any of them. It would be more helpful for him to know what his mother's rule is so that he can apply it to whatever particular circumstances surround his present desire for ice cream. Therefore, you would use the prior experiences to characterize more generally the factors that will likely influence his mother's decision in the future. Based on those experiences, his mother seems inclined to allow ice cream when he is at a special event, he is well-behaved, and he has eaten his entire meal. This is the synthesized rule. You would use this rule to explain to the child when he will likely be treated to ice cream again.

In a legal example, the prior experiences are the cases on point. The rule is synthesized from those cases and, to be useful, should not be limited to the facts of the cases. Rather, similar to the rule synthesized in the ice cream example, it should be stated generally so that it can be used to resolve future problems on the same issue.

Returning to synthesizing a legal rule for Mr. Gerardi's problem, let's suppose that we find four leading cases on the meaning of the word "dangerous" in the context of the state's dog biting statute. They include:

## The Dog Scratcher Case

Defendant was walking her dog without a leash or muzzle on a public sidewalk when the dog, without provocation, scratched a pedestrian. Defendant testified that her dog often gets "excitable" around strangers. She further testified that the dog never injured another person before this incident. The court therefore finds that Defendant is not in violation of this state's statute and thus not responsible for Plaintiff's medical expenses.

## The Dog Attacker Case

Defendant's dog bit Plaintiff, a neighbor, while the dog was allowed to roam freely, unleashed, on the public street. The dog was unprovoked. Plaintiff produced evidence showing that Defendant's dog attacked another person under similar circumstances just six months earlier. The injuries to that person were extensive; she suffered several deep lacerations that required over 30 stitches to her face and arms and eventual cosmetic surgery. Defendant was aware of that previous attack. Therefore, Defendant acted in violation of the statute when he did not leash or muzzle his dangerous dog. As a result, Defendant must pay Plaintiff's medical expenses.

## The Dog Biter Case

Defendant's dog bit Plaintiff while unleashed on a public street. Plaintiff produced a witness who testified that she was previously injured by Defendant's dog. During that prior incident, Defendant's dog had barked at the witness and jumped up on her legs, causing her to fall and scrape her knees. There were no other previous incidents with the dog. Because this prior incident was so minor, Defendant's dog was not "dangerous" within the meaning of the statute. Defendant is therefore not responsible for Plaintiff's medical expenses.

## The Killer Dog Case

Defendant's dog was unleashed and unmuzzled on a public street when it brutally attacked Plaintiff. There is no question that Defendant is responsible for paying Plaintiff's medical expenses as this same dog maimed someone two years earlier in another unprovoked attack. This dog falls squarely within the definition of "dangerous". It has a killer instinct. This is the precise type of injury this statute was intended to protect against.

There are several techniques that facilitate synthesizing rules from a series of cases like these. One is to group together the like cases—cases with similar holdings—and to compare the facts and reasoning of those cases to one another. In this example, the courts in *The Dog Attacker* and *The Killer Dog* cases both found that the defendants were responsible for the injuries their dogs caused whereas the courts in *The Dog Scratcher* and *The Dog Biter* cases did not. Thus, when re-reading and dissecting what happened in the cases, you would group them in this way.

Another useful tool is to chart the cases so that you can better see what is similar in the like cases and different about the other ones. The value of charting cases is explored in greater depth in a later chapter. For now, the easiest way to chart cases is to devote a column to each of the essential parts of a case; they include the relevant facts, holding (i.e., decision on the issue), and reasoning. If we were to group and then chart the dog cases, here is what the chart would look like:

| Case Name | Facts | Holding "Dangerous" Dog? | Reasoning |
|---|---|---|---|
| The Dog Attacker | Dog injured another person 6 months earlier; she suffered several deep lacerations that required over 30 stitches to her face and arms and eventual cosmetic surgery | ✓ | The injuries in prior incident were extensive |
| The Killer Dog | Dog maimed another person 2 years earlier | ✓ | Dog has "killer instinct"; precise type of injury statute intended to protect |
| The Dog Scratcher | Dog gets excitable around strangers but no prior injuries | No | No prior incidents that resulted in injuries; getting excited around strangers not enough |
| The Dog Biter | Prior incident in which dog barked and jumped on another's legs, causing that person to fall and scrape knees | No | Dog did not injure the person directly; injuries were very minor |

The chart helps us quickly see the facts that are present (or absent) in the like cases and what impact those facts had on each court's decision. The most significant fact in *The Dog Attacker* and *The Killer Dog* cases is that both dogs injured someone previously in unprovoked attacks. The time that passed since the prior unprovoked attacks seems immaterial because one of the attacks happened just 6 months earlier whereas the other one was 2 years earlier. Thus, the emphasis seems to be on the fact that the dog had a prior history of unprovoked attacks, not on how long ago those attacks happened. The second fact common to both cases and discussed in the courts' reasoning was that the prior injuries were extremely serious.

The similarity between *The Dog Scratcher* and *The Dog Biter* cases is that there were no prior unprovoked attacks. Though the dog in *The Dog Biter* case had caused an injury before, it was not the result of an attack, but rather playful dog behavior (jumping up on a stranger's leg). That behavior indirectly led to an injury when the person fell and scraped her knees. The injury there was also not severe.

Notice what facts did not appear in the chart. Omitted are the facts that were irrelevant to the disputed issue of whether the dog was dangerous, such as whether the dog was on public property and whether the dog was leashed or muzzled. Also purposefully excluded was the court's disposition of each case—that is, the ruling on whether the defendant was liable to pay the plaintiff's medical expenses. Thus, in synthesizing the rule, you will analyze only those facts and reasoning relevant to the disputed issue; all other information is irrelevant and therefore can drop out of the analysis.

After studying the chart, it becomes clear that courts will look at whether the dog has previously injured another person in an unprovoked attack and the extent of those injuries. In the absence of a prior incident resulting in serious injuries caused directly from an attack, a dog that injures another person when unprovoked will not be considered a "dangerous dog" within the meaning of the statute. Moreover, the existence of a prior incident in which normal playful dog behavior results in a minor injury to another is insufficient on its own to establish dangerousness. This is the synthesized rule. This is the rule we will apply to Mr. Gerardi's current situation— the third step to legal analysis.

In applying the rule, we will have to assess whether the prior incident in which Mr. Gerardi's dog injured a stranger fits the conditions for dangerousness. The prior incident did not involve an unprovoked attack, but rather a scratch, which is typical of dogs, even gentle ones, and akin to a dog's excitement around strangers, as in *The Dog Scratcher* case. Moreover, the incident resulted in a very minor injury—a scratch—similar in degree to the scraped knees in *The Dog Biter* case. It did not result in any serious harm, like the maiming and extensive lacerations in *The Killer Dog* and *The Dog Attacker* cases. In other words, Mr. Gerardi's situation is most similar to the facts in *The Dog Scratcher* and *The Dog Biter* cases and very distinguishable from *The Dog Attacker* and *The Killer Dog* cases. Therefore, because the conditions needed for establishing dangerousness are absent, Mr. Gerardi's dog is likely not a "dangerous" dog within the meaning of the statute. This prediction for how a court would likely resolve the disputed issue completes the fourth and final step to legal analysis.

If you refer back to Mr. Gerardi's question, however, he did not ask whether his dog was dangerous. Instead, he wanted to know whether he would have to pay the medical expenses of the injured child. The answer to that question requires that we pull together the answers to all of the issues it raised—both the undisputed and disputed ones. Though the dog was on public property, unleashed and unmuzzled, the dog is not a "dangerous" dog within the meaning of the statute. Because dangerousness is an essential element of the statute, its absence is fatal to the parents' demand for reimbursement of their child's medical expenses. In summary, Mr. Gerardi did nothing unlawful in letting his dog off his private property without a leash or muzzle. Hence, he is not liable for the child's injuries and does not need to pay the medical bill.

## How Law School Instruction Fits In

The process used in answering Mr. Gerardi's question is legal analysis in a nutshell. That is what law school teaches you to do across a spectrum of subject matters and, over time, with more complex law and facts. Mr. Gerardi's question allowed us to quickly walk through a simplified illustration of legal analysis. We will re-visit each step to legal analysis in greater depth in the later chapters. For now, it is important for you to understand the process at a high level so that you appreciate how the design of law school is intended to make you skilled in every step of it.

Your class reading and briefing of individual cases will give you practice in spotting issues and isolating relevant facts, holdings, and reasoning—the necessary foundation to building rules. For the most part, you will be working with rules that are not stated expressly in statutes or case law. Thus, you will be reading or discussing a handful of cases on each topic you cover and synthesizing rules from them. The hypothetical questions presented by your casebook, professors in class, and peers in your study groups will give you practice in applying those rules to new fact scenarios and making the appropriate predictions. Though class instruction and study group discussion should bring all of it together for you, your outlining will formally do so. As we will discuss more later, your outline will roadmap how to analyze any legal issue in a particular subject matter, as it will include the relevant issues, corresponding rules, and illustrations of how courts have resolved those issues in the past and their basis for doing so. Finally, your legal writing assignments and exams will test your ability to complete all steps of the process and effectively communicate your analysis in writing.

# Chapter 1 Exercise:

In February 2009, Carla Nash was mauled by a 200-pound pet male chimpanzee when he escaped from his Connecticut home.[2]  The chimpanzee, known as Travis, was fourteen-years-old at the time and had lived with his owner, Sandra Herold, since he was a child.  She treated him like a family member, feeding him steak, shrimp, and ice cream and even allowing him to sleep in her bed at times.  He was well-known in town because he had appeared in television commercials and photographs.  He was also very skilled in human activities; for example, he could drink wine from a stemmed glass, dress and bathe himself, and use a computer.

Travis had escaped before, and in 2003, playfully held up traffic at an intersection for several hours.  But he had no prior history of violence.  On the day of the attack, however, Travis was acting noticeably rambunctious.  In fact, Ms. Herold admitted to giving him the anti-anxiety drug Xanax earlier in the day to relax him.

Ms. Nash's injuries were near-fatal, as the chimpanzee ferociously bit at her face and hands.  Her injuries included the loss of both of her hands, plus her nose, lips, eyelids, and the bones in her mid-face.  The injuries were so bad that she was put in a medically induced coma for months.

By way of background, chimpanzees are very powerful and aggressive animals.  An average adult male has four to five times the upper body strength of an adult human.  Thus, even though they might seem harmless and even kind when babies, they should not be kept as pets.  In fact, it is not uncommon for chimpanzees to act aggressively toward their owners as they get older.

Assume that Ms. Nash has sought your services and would like to know whether she can sue Ms. Herold for her injuries, including her tremendous pain and suffering.  In answering her question, complete the following exercises:

1.  After some preliminary research into Connecticut state law, you locate a statute that states the following:

---

[2] This exercise is based on true events.  *See* Andy Newman and Anahad O'Connor, *Woman Mauled by Chimp Is Still in Critical Condition,* New York Times, February 17, 2009.  However, the law is fictitious so as to best illustrate the steps to legal analysis.

The owner of a wild animal is strictly liable[3] for any injuries that animal causes to another, even if the owner has exercised the utmost care to prevent the animal from doing harm.

- State the issue raised by Ms. Nash's question to you.

2. Suppose that the statute further defines "wild animal" to include "chimpanzees, tigers, pythons and other *ferae naturae*."

   a. Is the issue you identified in Question 1 a disputed or undisputed one? Explain your answer.

   b. How will a Connecticut court likely resolve the question of liability?

3. Now assume that the Connecticut statute instead states the following:

   The owner of an animal that has dangerous propensities is strictly liable for any injuries the animal causes to another, even if the owner has exercised the utmost care to prevent the animal from doing harm.

   a. State the issue raised by Ms. Nash's question to you.

   b. Is the issue a disputed or undisputed one? Explain your answer.

---

[3] A rule specifying strict liability makes a person legally responsible for the injuries regardless of culpability.

c. What steps will you take to resolve the issue?

d. What factual arguments can you make in favor and against Travis having "dangerous propensities"?

4. Using the Connecticut statute from Question 3, read the following three cases on the issue of "dangerous propensities" and answer the subsequent questions.

## The Bearded Dragon Lizard

Plaintiff was injured when Defendant's bearded dragon lizard nipped his finger. For those of you unfamiliar with this type of animal, the bearded dragon lizard has recently become a popular pet among teens and college students primarily because it is an attractive animal that is easy to care for, affordable, and very safe. Its rich, earth-tone coloration is, by lizard standards, simply beautiful. The lizard is native to Australia and commonly found in its deserts, but it is perfectly content when caged. Also, though it is fearsome-looking when its beard is puffed out, it is actually quite gentle-spirited. It not only adapts well to humans, but it enjoys their company. Other than an occasional bite when feeding, this animal is not naturally aggressive or harmful at any age. Therefore, Defendant is not liable for the injuries his dragon caused Plaintiff.

## The Lion Cub

Plaintiff was injured when Defendant's lion cub bit her several times on her leg, requiring over 30 stitches. Defendant raised the lion cub in his home, treating him very much like his baby. For example, he was bottle fed, bathed every night, and often cuddled on the couch with Defendant and his three young children. Though lion cubs are tame in their infancy and exhibit many attributes of a domesticated pet like a cat or dog, they are nonetheless wild animals. With age, they naturally become frustrated in captivity and, as a consequence, more aggressive. Biting is instinctive and, as seen here, can be very dangerous. Because a lion cub is a wild animal, it necessarily has dangerous propensities. Therefore, Defendant must pay Plaintiff's medical expenses.

## The Gator

Plaintiff was injured by Defendant's pet alligator. The alligator, which was 4 ½ feet in length and weighed approximately 180 pounds, escaped Defendant's property through a large hole in his fence. It viscously attacked Plaintiff, a neighbor, while she was gardening outside. Plaintiff suffered serious injuries to her face, hands, arms, and legs. Plaintiff seeks reimbursement for her medical bills and immense pain and suffering. This case is an easy one. There is no question that an alligator is a dangerous animal. It is wild and thus by its very nature is ferocious. Even in its infancy, an alligator has the potential to harm. However, certainly when it reaches adulthood, as is the case here, any animal—human or otherwise—that nears it is potential prey. In fact, they are known to eat wild boars, deer, dogs, and even livestock. That is precisely why they should not be kept as pets. Accordingly, Defendant is liable.

a.  First, chart the cases. Devote a column to the essential parts of each case; the essential parts include the relevant facts, holding (i.e., decision on the issue), and reasoning.

b.  Second, synthesize a rule for "dangerous propensities." In other words, what do courts consider in deciding whether an animal has "dangerous propensities"?

c.   Third, apply your rule to the problem.   Does Travis, the chimpanzee, have "dangerous propensities"? If you decide that Travis has "dangerous propensities", explain why he is similar to the animals in *The Lion Cub* and *The Gator* cases and dissimilar to the animal in *The Bearded Dragon Lizard* case.   If you decide that Travis does not have "dangerous propensities", explain why he is similar to the animal in *The Bearded Dragon Lizard* case and dissimilar to the animals in *The Lion Cub* and *The Gator* cases.

d.   Finally, using your analysis, answer Ms. Nash's original question.   Will Ms. Herold be liable to pay Ms. Nash's medical expenses?

# The Essential Skill: Reading Cases

Much of what you do in law school is read judicial opinions or what lawyers colloquially refer to as cases. In fact, it is not uncommon for professors to assign fifty to a hundred pages of reading on a single topic, most of which is in the form of edited judicial opinions or notes cases. (Notes cases are simply abbreviated discussions of judicial opinions in the editor's notes following the main judicial opinions on that topic.) Professors will not only expect that you read all of the material in advance of class, but also that you prepare detailed notes on what you have read. Your notes on the cases are what law professors call case briefs. We will discuss how to effectively brief a case in the next chapter. For now, you should know that professors expect you to bring your notes or case briefs to class so that you can actively participate in class discussions.

## What Happens in Class: Cases and The Socratic Method

In class, professors will talk about what happened in the individual cases and how they relate to each other. Many will do so by employing a style of teaching known as the Socratic method.[4] Professors who use the Socratic method typically will not lecture on the law. Instead, they will teach the law by soliciting students' answers to a series of questions about the cases they assigned as well as by asking them to resolve hypothetical scenarios ("hypos") that address the same topic as the assigned cases but involve a slightly different set of circumstances. Essentially, professors use specific examples (in the form of cases or hypos) to teach general legal concepts. Some professors will ask for volunteers to answer their questions while others might be more traditional and "cold call" on students (that is, call on them randomly). In either event, professors use the question-answer exchange to

---

[4] This style of teaching is named after Socrates, the Athenian philosopher who taught his students through questioning, not lecture, on the theory that they would discover the "truth" together.

push students to work through the individual cases and develop the law on a particular topic on their own.

Thus, it is unwise to passively sit through class, even when you are not the one "on call", as you could easily miss how the cases build on one another and relate to the broader legal concepts. To stay engaged in your classroom learning, you should pay close attention to the questions and try to answer all of them, even if only silently. You should take good notes on what comes out of the discussions as well. In the end, you are expected to bring together or synthesize your case briefs and class notes into an outline of the course. That outline, discussed at length in Chapter 4, will need to illustrate not only the specific legal points covered by the cases but also the general legal concepts, their corresponding rules, as well as their applications to different fact scenarios. Though all of this is eventually developed in class, the professor will not organize or summarize it for you in a single, written outline covering the entire course.

You must create your own outline of the course. Using the professor's syllabus or table of contents in the casebook as guidance on the skeletal structure of the outline, you must ultimately figure out where and how the specifics of what you read and learned in class fit in and then expand it appropriately. Because the cases are the starting point in this long process, your ability to read cases effectively is an essential part of your law school learning.

## A Quick Detour . . . Does This Method of Teaching Work?

You might wonder whether this method of teaching makes any sense. In fact, for most of you, it is contrary to the way your undergraduate teaching was structured, where general concepts were introduced before specific ones and professors even outlined or summarized the material for you in some fashion. It certainly would be less stressful on you if law professors did the same and shared their outline of the course material before, or at least, concurrent with your learning it. Then, instead of dissecting the cases one by one, they could spend class time explaining what each part of the outline meant and how the cases fit into it. If your courses were laid out this way, all you would need to do is memorize the pertinent rules and recall how they worked in the assigned cases so that you could apply them to future ones.

Despite these apparent benefits, this approach is significantly flawed in that it fails to really teach you how to think like a lawyer—the goal of law school. Memorizing legal rules without first understanding how they developed and why they were applied in the way they were is not the best way to learn how to analyze legal problems—the job of a practicing lawyer. Rather, the best way is for you to labor through the reading and synthesis of the cases so that you learn the law, understand the relationship between different legal rules on the same topic, and see their connection to the broader, more general concepts.

## Why You Read Cases in Law School: The Connection to Practice

Because you need to be skilled in analyzing legal problems to practice law, in law school, you read actual cases, rather than textbooks that summarize the law. By reading cases, you learn to see patterns in how courts resolve like problems and develop rules from those patterns that are applicable to future scenarios. In practice, when an attorney is faced with a legal problem, he or she does not usually find the answer in a single source. Rather, that attorney must research and understand the applicable law in the relevant jurisdiction as it relates to the specific circumstances of the problem. In most cases, the attorney's research begins by reading cases on the topic.

If the problem were to involve a contracts claim, for example, that attorney would not rely solely on his or her law school casebook or course outline from contracts or any other legal secondary authority for that matter to see how the problem should be resolved. The answer would not be there. It is simply impossible for a single course or resource to cover every potential contracts question that could arise and the relevant law of all jurisdictions. While the cases and lessons from a contracts course or a secondary authority might give an attorney ideas on how to approach the particular problem, that attorney must be skilled in reading cases and analyzing legal problems on his or her own to actually resolve the client's problem competently.

Accordingly, the reading you do in law school prepares you for a career in problem-solving. Law professors try to simulate what happens in law practice when they ask you to resolve actual or hypothetical problems using what you learned from the cases you previously read on the subject. Their hope is that over time you will be able to read cases on any issue, synthesize a rule from them, and apply that rule appropriately and convincingly to whatever legal problem you might face as a practicing lawyer.

## Reading with a Purpose

The preceding background on how cases are used to teach the law as well as critical analytical thinking skills is intended to shape how you go about reading cases in law school. Too many students, especially first-years, approach reading cases in a vacuum. They forget the "big picture" and thus read simply to finish the assignment and prepare for class. If they think about outlining, they do so only in a limited way, concerned mostly about the mechanics of filling one in. As you now know, a model outline is more than a summary of your case briefs and class notes; it synthesizes the cases and illustrates how lawyers resolve the legal issues raised by the course. Only through a focused reading of the cases will you be able to build such a model outline.

The most important parts of a judicial opinion are the issue, the legally relevant facts, the court's holding, and rationale.

Thus, you need to read cases with the clear purpose of extracting only the information that helps you in this regard. At a minimum, that information includes the question or issue the court has been asked to resolve, the court's holding on that issue, the legally relevant facts, and the court's rationale. These are the most important parts of a judicial opinion and, for that reason, are explained in great depth below.

## The Anatomy of a Judicial Opinion: The Issue

A judicial opinion is a court's written decision on a legal question. The legal question is commonly referred to as *the legal issue* or simply *the issue*. Thus,

when your law professors ask what the issue in a
case was, they are asking you to state the legal
question that was before the court. There are two
types of legal questions that you will encounter in
your reading—substantive ones and procedural ones.

*The issue is the legal question that the court must answer.*

Substantive legal questions address the rights, duties, powers and liabilities of
people and entities. An example of a substantive legal question is whether a
defendant is strictly liable for injuries caused to another by his dog. (This is the
question your client, Mr. Gerardi, had sought advice on in Chapter 1.) Procedural
legal questions, on the other hand, concern the rules by which courts hear and
determine what happens in a case. An example of a procedural legal question is
whether a court has jurisdiction (that is, legal power) to decide a lawsuit. For
instance, in Mr. Gerardi's case, if the injury took place in New York, but the boy's
parents filed a complaint against Mr. Gerardi in a New Jersey state court, there
might be a question as to whether the New Jersey court has jurisdiction over the
parties.

Some questions involve a combination of substantive and procedural law. An
example, also on the topic of a dog owner's liability, is whether a plaintiff has
demonstrated a triable issue of material fact on the issue of a dog's vicious
propensities to defeat a motion for summary judgment[5]. (This is the mixed legal
question raised in the *Miletich* decision at the end of this chapter.) Because the
court necessarily must address the substantive law of a dog owner's liability in
deciding whether the plaintiff has satisfied its procedural burden, it is a mixed
question of substance and procedure. In addition to mixed questions, some cases
might address more than a single legal question. For pedagogical reasons,
however, most casebooks are edited so that the opinions you read reflect a court's
decision on a single question only.

Additionally, legal questions may be fact-based or purely legal in nature. The
examples above are fact-based because they require that the court examine how

---

[5] A motion for summary judgment asks the court to decide the case (or a portion of it) without a full trial.
To prevail on such a motion, the moving party must establish that there are no issues of material fact
requiring a trial for their resolution and that in applying the law to the undisputed facts the moving party is
clearly entitled to judgment in its favor.

the law applies to a particular fact scenario. In contrast, a purely legal question can be answered without looking at the facts of a particular case. An example is whether a statute that makes a dog owner strictly liable for any injuries caused by his or her dog is constitutional. Because you do not need to know anything about the dog, the owner, or the injuries to decide whether such a law is permissible, the question is a purely legal one. Most of the cases you will read in law school or deal with in practice will be fact-based, however. Therefore, the examples in this book focus on these types of questions exclusively.

Regardless of the type, the legal question that the court must resolve is the most significant part of the case as all other aspects center on answering that question. Therefore, you will want to identify the legal question early on in your reading. When the court explicitly states the question by saying something like "the issue before us" or "the question this Court must decide is . . .," your job is a fairly easy one. However, oftentimes, the question is not introduced in such a helpful fashion; rather, it is implicit from the court's holding. When that is the case, you will obviously need to take a closer look at what the court did to isolate and frame the question. Once you have done that though, peeling away at the remaining layers of the opinion is usually straightforward.

## The Anatomy of a Judicial Opinion: The Facts, Holding, and Rationale

The court's answer to the legal question is the holding. If a court were to decide that Mr. Gerardi is liable for the injuries his dog caused to the young boy, for example, that would be its holding—its answer to the substantive, fact-based legal question raised by the problem. Similarly, if a court were to decide that a statute that makes a dog owner strictly liable for any injuries caused by his or her dog is constitutional, that would be its holding—its answer to the purely legal substantive question. Finally, the holding on the mixed legal question in the *Miletich* decision at the end of the chapter is that the plaintiff failed to demonstrate a triable issue of material fact on the issue of the dog's vicious propensities.

A court's reasoning or support for its decision is the rationale. Reasoning might include public policy, social concerns, and legislative intent, among other things.

Knowing why a court applied the law in the way it did is important to figuring out whether it should be applied similarly or differently in future cases.

Finally, the facts of a case tell what happened between the parties that led to their dispute. Every case has a story—an explanation as to who the parties are and the basis for the legal action. Not all facts matter, though. There are legally significant or relevant facts. These are the facts that the court relied on in reaching its decision or holding. These are the most important ones. Then, there are the background or supporting facts. These are facts that give meaning to the story or help explain the relevant ones, but were not a necessary part of the court's decision. In other words, their presence did not influence the court's decision on the issue in any material way. Oftentimes you will find the facts of a case at the beginning of the opinion. However, because courts apply rules to the facts in reaching their holdings, it is not uncommon to see a more in-depth or detailed discussion of the facts when the court explains its reasoning. The *Miletich* decision at the end of this chapter gives an example of this.

## The Anatomy of a Judicial Opinion: The Other Parts

Though the issue, facts, holding, and reasoning are the essence of a judicial opinion, there are other parts that are also useful to understanding the court's decision and its likely impact on future cases. At the very top of every judicial decision is the case caption. The caption identifies the names of the parties and their positions in the lawsuit. If it is a decision by a trial court, the designations plaintiff and defendant will be used. If there is more than one plaintiff or defendant, you might see "*et al.*" following a name. It is the Latin term for "and others", meaning there are other parties to the lawsuit, but they are not named individually in order to save space. If it is a decision by an appellate court, the designations appellant and appellee or petitioner and respondent (depending on the jurisdiction) will be used. The caption also identifies the name of the court that decided the case. The citation to the case, which indicates the reporter (book) or reporters in which the case can be found and exactly where in that reporter the case appears (volume and page), is immediately above the caption.[6]

Immediately following the caption is the name of the judge who authored the opinion. An appellate court opinion is usually decided by a panel of judges. A unanimous decision is one in which all of the judges agree on the result in the case and the reasons for it. If the judges cannot all agree, the majority's opinion is what becomes law. When a judge disagrees with the result, he or she dissents. That judge, along with others, might also write a dissenting opinion, explaining why they disagree with the majority's opinion. When a judge agrees with the result, but does not fully agree with the court's reason for it, he or she might write a concurring opinion. Both dissenting and concurring opinions have no binding effect on future cases, though they are always instructive on the meaning of the law and many times help shape change. If there are such opinions, they would appear after the majority one and the judges who join in those opinions would be listed with them.

The opinion itself begins after the name of the judge who authored it. Though there is no set template for how opinions are written, the issue, facts, holding, and reasoning are generally presented in that order. At the very beginning, however, there is usually a discussion of the procedural history of the case. The procedural history explains the history of the case leading up to the decision at hand. If it is an appeals decision, it will tell what happened in the lower court proceedings and then explain the current procedural posture of the case. For example, it might be the motion that the court is deciding or the basis for the appeal.

The disposition of the case is typically next. The disposition is the action that the court decided to take based on its decision. If the procedural posture is an appeal, the appellate court may find that the lower court's decision was correct and therefore *affirm* the decision. If the appellate court were to find that the decision of

---

[6] The citation to the *Miletich* decision later in this chapter can be explained as follows. It is a parallel citation because the decision can be found in more than one reporter. The number that precedes the reporter abbreviation is the volume of that reporter and the number that follows the reporter abbreviation is the first page number in that reporter. Thus, the *Miletich* decision can be found in Volume 70 of the Appellate Division Reports Third Series beginning on page 1095 as well as in Volume 895 of the West's New York Supplement Second Series beginning on page 557. Table 1 of the Bluebook, which lists jurisdictional information for the federal and state level (alphabetically) provides a listing of the court information of each jurisdiction as well as the full title of the reporters. It is useful in anchoring yourself. *See infra* at p. 30 (*Anchoring Yourself*).

the lower court was incorrect, it would *reverse* the decision.[7] The affirmance and reversal are examples of a court's disposition. For lower court decisions, the disposition will be the court's ruling on the issue. For example, if the procedural posture is a motion to dismiss the complaint, the disposition is the granting or denial of such a motion. The disposition is usually stated again at the conclusion of the opinion.

Students often confuse the disposition of the case with the court's holding. Remember the holding is the court's resolution of the issue. The disposition is what happens to the parties based on its resolution. If a court were to find that Mr. Gerardi's dog is dangerous, it would then order Mr. Gerardi to pay the injured child's medical expenses. The ruling on dangerousness would be the holding. The holding, as discussed earlier, is what matters for figuring out how courts will resolve future cases on the same issue. The practical result for the parties involved — Mr. Gerardi compensating the child for his injuries — would be the disposition. Because the disposition has no impact on future cases, it plays no role in rule synthesis and outlining.

The applicable law usually follows the procedural history and disposition of the case. It is the law that the court examines and uses in reaching its ruling. It might include statutes, constitutions or prior decisions. This section is usually very illuminating because it explains what rule the court is applying to its decision. If there is prior authority that establishes a rule or principle on the same or similar issue and facts — what lawyers refer to as precedent — the court will discuss it here. This section also gives insight into how the court will reconcile its decision with the prior precedent — in other words, how the court will apply the precedent rule to its case.

---

[7] Students sometimes confuse the terminology reverse with overrule. When a higher court disagrees with a lower court's decision on the same case, it is reversing, not overruling that decision. A decision of a higher or equal court at a later point in time and involving another case would overrule an earlier decision if it reached a different result on virtually the same set of facts. Essentially that later court is deciding that a previous rule was wrong. For example, in 2011, if the New York Court of Appeals decided that dog owners are strictly liable for injuries their dogs cause only under certain circumstances, namely knowledge of their dog's vicious propensities, that decision would overrule an earlier 2010 decision by that court or a lower court that made dog owners strictly liable for injuries their dogs caused no matter what the circumstances.

# A Quick Detour. . . Understanding the Organization of the United States Court System

You need to know how the United States court system is organized in order to fully understand what, if any impact, precedent will have on a court's decision. Generally, there is a three-tiered hierarchy of the courts at both the state and federal level. At the state level, there are trial courts (the lower courts), intermediate appellate courts, and the highest appellate courts, which are usually referred to as Supreme Courts.[8] At the federal level, there are also trial courts; they are called United States District Courts. There is one for each of the 94 federal districts in the United States. Every state has at least one district, with some states, like New York[9], having multiple districts. The government website www.uscourts.gov has a map outlining the district divisions.

The federal appellate courts are called United States Courts of Appeals or Circuit Courts. The 94 judicial districts are divided into 12 regional circuits, each of which has a United States Court of Appeals. A Court of Appeals will hear appeals from the district courts located within its circuit as well as appeals from decisions of federal administrative agencies. The United States Supreme Court is the highest court at the federal level. The Supreme Court consists of a Chief Justice and eight associate justices. The Supreme Court only hears a limited number of cases each year, usually involving significant questions about the Constitution or federal law.

## Applicable Law and the Principle of Stare Decisis

As you will learn in your first few weeks of law school, judges are supposed to follow the principle of *stare decisis* when deciding cases. *Stare decisis*, a short form of the Latin phrase *stare decisis et non quieta movere,* means "to stand by precedents and not to disturb settled principles of law." According to this principle, judges should follow the rulings of earlier decisions involving facts substantially similar to the ones before them. The theory is that the law will be applied more

---

[8] Though New York State's highest court is the New York Court of Appeals. The lower court is New York Supreme Court and the intermediate appellate courts are the New York Appellate Division courts (1st, 2nd, 3rd and 4th departments).
[9] New York has four districts—Southern, Northern, Western, and Eastern.

consistently and fairly if judges abide by precedent. If judges were allowed to decide cases without regard to prior authority on the same issue, there would be great disparity in how the law was applied. This disparity could create a very unpredictable and unstable legal system.

The principle of *stare decisis* has two more related components. The first is the rule that a decision by a higher court in a jurisdiction is binding precedent (also known as mandatory authority) on an inferior court in that same jurisdiction. For example, a decision by the New York Court of Appeals—the highest court in New York—on the issue of a dog's viscous propensities would be binding on a New York Appellate Division court or the New York Supreme Court because they are both inferior courts within the same state jurisdiction. Decisions by an inferior court, however, are not binding on a higher court within a jurisdiction. As a consequence, the lower courts cannot change the law established by their high court. Therefore, the New York Court of Appeals is not bound by a decision by the New York Appellate Division or New York Supreme Court. A decision by either court might be persuasive authority, but not mandatory authority on the high court. Similarly, decisions by a court outside of the jurisdiction would have only a persuasive effect on a court within the jurisdiction. For instance, if a case is before a New York court—any New York court for that matter—decisions by a New Jersey court (even by its highest court) or the federal courts would not be binding on the New York court; they would have a persuasive effect only.

The second component to the principle of *stare decisis* is that a court should not overturn or change its own precedents unless it has a strong reason to do so. Therefore, the New York Court of Appeals should not regularly change its mind on issues, as this would create instability. Though the principle of *stare decisis* is the foundation of our common law system, it is not always rigidly followed. Judges can, and often do, distinguish their cases from previous ones when there are differences in the facts, allowing them to deviate from precedent. It is important for judges to have this flexibility in order to accommodate changing circumstances. When judges distinguish their cases from prior ones or discuss how their cases are similar to prior ones, they are reasoning by analogy. They are distinguishing or analogizing the cases depending on the circumstances. When reasoning by analogy, they are following the principles of *stare decisis.* To the extent they are unable to stand by a prior decision on a similar set of facts, they are justifying why they cannot.

Thus, applicable law is very useful in understanding the purpose behind a current rule of law and how it will be applied in future cases. This part of the opinion is often quite lengthy and is easily identifiable by its citations to other decisions and authority. The citations themselves provide insight into whether the authority is binding or just persuasive on the deciding court. It is helpful to think of this part of the opinion as the court's justification for its decision to either follow or deviate from precedent. Either way, it is important to understand and study, as you will need to similarly explain your answers to the legal questions you will be asked to resolve.

## Anchoring Yourself

In addition to knowing the general anatomy of a judicial decision, an important precursor to the actual reading of cases is anchoring yourself—that is, familiarizing yourself with the case you are about to read and removing any barriers that might prevent your complete understanding of it. Anchoring yourself requires that you learn as much background information on the topic of the case and the court that decided it so that you can read the case with a clear focus, not blindly. Part of this anchoring is seeing where the case appears in the casebook. You can use the course syllabus and the casebook table of contents and headings to figure out the general and specific topics under which the case falls.

For example, the *Miletich* decision at the end of this chapter, would probably be in your Torts casebook under the main topic Strict Liability and under the sub-topics Pet Owner's Liability, under Dogs, and then under "Dangerous" or "Viscous Propensities". Knowing these headings clue you in to the main subject of the case before you even read it. The caption itself is another place to find useful context. It tells you a lot about who the parties are, the procedural posture of the case, which court decided the case, and the year of the decision, facts that can reveal, among other things, what political or social influences might have affected the court's decision.

Only after you have gathered background information on the opinion should you read it for the first time. During your initial read, it is imperative that you do not take notes on it; you should read it without a writing utensil or computer in hand. You need to read the case once through before you can appreciate what issue the court was deciding, its reasoning, and what the relevant facts were. This is particularly true when it comes to the facts because many facts seem important early on. However, it is only the relevant facts— the ones the court relied on in reaching its decision—that actually matter. You will not know what those are until you have read the entire decision without breaking. If you mark up the case in your casebook or take notes on it prematurely, you will likely record or highlight irrelevant information while disregarding or overlooking relevant information. It is too time consuming to redo your notes. In the case of markings on the text itself, they may even be impossible to erase. Therefore, acquaint yourself with the case by reading it for the very first time without taking any notes or marking it up in any way.

*You should read a case the first time through without a writing utensil in hand or computer by your side. Highlighting text and taking notes during the first read almost always yields irrelevant and incomplete information. Relying on that information could negatively impact your case briefing.*

After you have read the case once, you should read it a second time for the sole purpose of translating or decoding any terms of art unfamiliar to you. In the beginning, there will be many words and legal terms of art that are foreign, particularly in the procedural history part of the decision. Rather than ignoring them or guessing at their significance so that you can move on quickly, assume they are essential to a complete understanding of the case and make it a point to learn the new vocabulary. Use a Black's Law Dictionary or an online law dictionary to translate unknown words. The best way to internalize the new vocabulary is to write the plain meaning of the words on the case itself; for example, you can circle the word in the text and bubble out its definition in the margins. With this written translation, you will be able to read the case the next time through in plain English.

# Annotating Cases

On your third read, at the earliest, is when you should begin annotating the decision. You will need to identify and mark in some fashion the different parts of the opinion. You can use different color highlighting or bracket the relevant text and identify the parts of the decision in the margins. The *Miletich* decision below is an unedited decision by a New York state appellate court. The court addressed the question of whether a dog owner was liable for injuries her dog caused to another. You should read the decision several times before taking any notes or making any markings on it. Then you should see if you can identify the main parts of the decision—the issue, facts, holding, and rationale—as well as the others parts—the caption, procedural history, applicable law, and disposition on your own. Following the decision is an annotated version of the same decision but in a table format. The annotations describe to what part of the decision the text corresponds. In the beginning, you should annotate cases in this way. Ultimately, you will want to choose whatever method best suits your needs. Whatever the method, your annotations of cases will be an essential building block for case briefing, the next step in the process.

---

70 A.D.3d 1095, 895 N.Y.S.2d 557

Supreme Court, Appellate Division, Third Department, New York.
Heidi J. MILETICH et al., Appellants,

v.

Christopher KOPP et al., Respondents.

Feb. 4, 2010.

MALONE Jr., J.

Appeal from an order of the Supreme Court (Demarest, J.), entered February 27, 2009 in Franklin County, which, among other things, granted defendants' motion for summary judgment dismissing the complaint.

Plaintiff Heidi J. Miletich (hereinafter plaintiff) and her husband, derivatively, commenced this action alleging that defendants' dog bit plaintiff. As plaintiff, a stranger to the dog, approached defendants' front door, the dog, which was tied nearby, bit her twice on her left leg and she either fell or was knocked to the ground, injuring her right wrist. Plaintiffs now appeal Supreme Court's dismissal of the complaint upon cross motions for summary judgment. We affirm.

"'[A] plaintiff may not recover for injuries sustained in an attack by a dog unless he or she establishes that the dog had vicious propensities and that its owner knew or should have known of such propensities'" (*Scheidt v. Oberg,* 65 A.D.3d 740, 740, 883 N.Y.S.2d 661 (2009), quoting *Palleschi v. Granger,* 13 A.D.3d 871, 872, 786 N.Y.S.2d 627 (2004); *see Collier v. Zambito,* 1 N.Y.3d 444, 446, 775 N.Y.S.2d 205, 807 N.E.2d 254 (2004); *Malpezzi v. Ryan,* 28 A.D.3d 1036, 1037, 815 N.Y.S.2d 295 (2006)). A dog's vicious propensities may be evidenced by prior vicious behavior such as biting, growling, snapping or baring its teeth, and an inference that the owner is aware of such a propensity may be raised where, for example, the dog is maintained as a guard dog or is restrained by the owner out of a concern that the dog will put others at risk of harm (*see Collier v. Zambito,* 1 N.Y.3d at 447, 775 N.Y.S.2d 205, 807 N.E.2d 254; *Illian v. Butler,* 66 A.D.3d 1312, 1313, 888 N.Y.S.2d 247 (2009); *Morse v. Colombo,* 8 A.D.3d 808, 809, 777 N.Y.S.2d 824 (2004)). The breed of a dog, alone, does not create a triable issue of fact as to the dog's propensities, but may be considered together with other factors (*see Loper v. Dennie,* 24 A.D.3d 1131, 1133, 807 N.Y.S.2d 672 (2005)).

Defendants satisfied their initial burden on summary judgment by submitting the transcripts of several examinations before trial establishing that defendants acquired the dog, a purebred Chow Chow, as a family pet when he was eight weeks old and owned him for approximately four years prior to the incident without knowledge of any vicious propensities (*see Scheidt v. Oberg,* 65 A.D.3d at 740, 883 N.Y.S.2d 661; *Blackstone v. Hayward,* 304 A.D.2d 941, 941, 757 N.Y.S.2d 160 (2003), *lv. Denied* 100 N.Y.2d 511, 766 N.Y.S.2d 164, 798 N.E.2d 348 (2003)). The burden then shifted to plaintiffs to demonstrate a triable issue of material fact, which plaintiffs failed to do (*see Malpezzi v. Ryan,* 28 A.D.3d at 1037, 815 N.Y.S.2d 295). Evidence that defendants routinely restrained the dog to keep him from running away does not support an inference that defendants were aware that the dog might pose a danger (*see Palleschi v. Granger,* 13 A.D.3d at 872, 786 N.Y.S.2d 627; *Campo v. Holland,* 32 A.D.3d 630, 632, 820 N.Y.S.2d 352 (2006)). Nor does evidence that the dog was "nippy" or "territorial" when he was just several weeks old raise a triable issue as to defendants' liability (*see Tessiero v. Conrad,* 186 A.D.2d 330, 330, 588 N.Y.S.2d 200 (1992); *compare Earl v. Piowaty,* 42 A.D.3d 865, 866, 839 N.Y.S.2d 861 (2007)). Defendant Christopher Kopp's testimony that he has seen the Chow Chow breed identified as potentially aggressive and was aware of incidences of aggressiveness involving that breed does not, by itself, create an issue of fact regarding defendants' knowledge of any vicious propensities in their dog (*see Malpezzi v. Ryan,* 28 A.D.3d at 1038, 815 N.Y.S.2d 295). Finally, the manner in which plaintiff was bitten does not support an inference that the dog was aggressive, where plaintiff never saw the dog until immediately before she was bitten and Kopp testified that the dog had been sleeping and was startled by plaintiff's presence (*see id.; Arcara v. Whytas,* 219 A.D.2d 871, 872, 632 N.Y.S.2d 349 (1995)). Accordingly, the complaint was properly dismissed.

ORDERED that the order is affirmed, with costs.

PETERS, J.P., ROSE, STEIN and McCARTHY, JJ., concur.

# Annotated *Miletich* Decision

| | |
|---|---|
| 70 A.D.3d 1095, 895 N.Y.S.2d 557 | Citation |
| Supreme Court, Appellate Division, Third Department, New York.<br>Heidi J. MILETICH et al., Appellants,<br>v.<br>Christopher KOPP et al., Respondents.<br><br>Feb. 4, 2010. | Caption |
| MALONE Jr., J. | Authoring Judge |
| Appeal from an order of the Supreme Court (Demarest, J.), entered February 27, 2009 in Franklin County, which, among other things, granted defendants' motion for summary judgment dismissing the complaint.<br><br>Plaintiff Heidi J. Miletich (hereinafter plaintiff) and her husband, derivatively, commenced this action alleging that defendants' dog bit plaintiff. | Procedural History |
| As plaintiff, a stranger to the dog, approached defendants' front door, the dog, which was tied nearby, bit her twice on her left leg and she either fell or was knocked to the ground, injuring her right wrist. | Relevant facts |
| Plaintiffs now appeal Supreme Court's dismissal of the complaint upon cross motions for summary judgment. | Procedural Posture |
| We affirm. | Disposition |
| "'[A] plaintiff may not recover for injuries sustained in an attack by a dog unless he or she establishes that the dog had vicious propensities and that its owner knew or should have known of such propensities'" (*Scheidt v. Oberg*, 65 A.D.3d 740, 740, 883 N.Y.S.2d 661 | Applicable Law<br>(precedent rules) |

| | |
|---|---|
| (2009), quoting *Palleschi v. Granger,* 13 A.D.3d 871, 872, 786 N.Y.S.2d 627 (2004); *see Collier v. Zambito,* 1 N.Y.3d 444, 446, 775 N.Y.S.2d 205, 807 N.E.2d 254 (2004); *Malpezzi v. Ryan,* 28 A.D.3d 1036, 1037, 815 N.Y.S.2d 295 (2006)). A dog's vicious propensities may be evidenced by prior vicious behavior such as biting, growling, snapping or baring its teeth, and an inference that the owner is aware of such a propensity may be raised where, for example, the dog is maintained as a guard dog or is restrained by the owner out of a concern that the dog will put others at risk of harm (*see Collier v. Zambito,* 1 N.Y.3d at 447, 775 N.Y.S.2d 205, 807 N.E.2d 254; *Illian v. Butler,* 66 A.D.3d 1312, 1313, 888 N.Y.S.2d 247 (2009); *Morse v. Colombo,* 8 A.D.3d 808, 809, 777 N.Y.S.2d 824 (2004)). The breed of a dog, alone, does not create a triable issue of fact as to the dog's propensities, but may be considered together with other factors (*see Loper v. Dennie,* 24 A.D.3d 1131, 1133, 807 N.Y.S.2d 672 (2005)). | |
| Defendants satisfied their initial burden on summary judgment by submitting the transcripts of several examinations before trial establishing that defendants acquired the dog, a purebred Chow Chow, as a family pet when he was eight weeks old and owned him for approximately four years prior to the incident without knowledge of any vicious propensities (*see Scheidt v. Oberg,* 65 A.D.3d at 740, 883 N.Y.S.2d 661; *Blackstone v. Hayward,* 304 A.D.2d 941, 941, 757 N.Y.S.2d 160 (2003), *lv. denied* 100 N.Y.2d 511, 766 N.Y.S.2d 164, 798 N.E.2d 348 (2003)). | Relevant facts |
| The burden then shifted to plaintiffs to demonstrate a triable issue of material fact, which plaintiffs failed to do (*see Malpezzi v. Ryan,* 28 A.D.3d at 1037, 815 N.Y.S.2d 295). | Issue & Holding |

| | |
|---|---|
| Evidence that defendants routinely restrained the dog to keep him from running away does not support an inference that defendants were aware that the dog might pose a danger (*see Palleschi v. Granger,* 13 A.D.3d at 872, 786 N.Y.S.2d 627; *Campo v. Holland,* 32 A.D.3d 630, 632, 820 N.Y.S.2d 352 (2006)). Nor does evidence that the dog was "nippy" or "territorial" when he was just several weeks old raise a triable issue as to defendants' liability (*see Tessiero v. Conrad,* 186 A.D.2d 330, 330, 588 N.Y.S.2d 200 (1992); *compare Earl v. Piowaty,* 42 A.D.3d 865, 866, 839 N.Y.S.2d 861 (2007)). Defendant Christopher Kopp's testimony that he has seen the Chow Chow breed identified as potentially aggressive and was aware of incidences of aggressiveness involving that breed does not, by itself, create an issue of fact regarding defendants' knowledge of any vicious propensities in their dog (*see Malpezzi v. Ryan,* 28 A.D.3d at 1038, 815 N.Y.S.2d 295). Finally, the manner in which plaintiff was bitten does not support an inference that the dog was aggressive, where plaintiff never saw the dog until immediately before she was bitten and Kopp testified that the dog had been sleeping and was startled by plaintiff's presence (*see id.; Arcara v. Whytas,* 219 A.D.2d 871, 872, 632 N.Y.S.2d 349 (1995)). | Relevant facts & Reasoning (application of precedent rules) |
| Accordingly, the complaint was properly dismissed. | Holding |
| ORDERED that the order is affirmed, with costs. | Disposition |
| PETERS, J.P., ROSE, STEIN and McCARTHY, JJ., concur. | Concurring Judges |

# Chapter 2 Exercise:

Read and annotate the below two cases by the New York Appellate Division using the following labels where applicable: Citation, Caption, Authoring Judge, Procedural History, Procedural Posture, Disposition, Applicable Law, Issue, Holding, Reasoning, Relevant or Background Facts, and Concurring Judges.

------------------------------------------------

66 A.D.3d 1312, 888 N.Y.S.2d 247

Supreme Court, Appellate Division, Third Department, New York.
Ann ILLIAN et al., Appellants,

v.

Gail BUTLER et al., Respondents.

Oct. 29, 2009.

GARRY, J.

Appeal from an order of the Supreme Court (Cahill, J.), entered July 11, 2008 in Ulster County, which granted defendants' motion for summary judgment dismissing the complaint.

In June 2005, while plaintiffs were temporarily residing at a campground in Accord, Ulster County, plaintiff Ann Illian (hereinafter plaintiff) was bitten by Sadie, a mixed-breed dog belonging to defendants, who also resided at the campground. Defendants and plaintiffs had known one another for years, and plaintiff was also well acquainted with the dog. Plaintiff testified that she had patted Sadie, played with her, and kissed her on numerous prior occasions without incident, and had once even taken her to the veterinarian. On the day of plaintiff's injury, she attended a party at defendants' campground residence to celebrate defendant Jeffrey Sloat's birthday. During the party, Sadie was tied by a chain on defendants' front porch, where plaintiff patted her once or twice in the course of the evening. Shortly before she was bitten, plaintiff left defendants' residence briefly. Upon her return, she reached out to pat Sadie as she climbed the porch steps. The dog lunged and bit plaintiff in the face.

Plaintiff and her husband, derivatively, commenced this action in May 2007. Defendants moved for summary judgment dismissing the complaint, contending that they neither knew nor should have known of the dog's vicious propensities. Supreme Court granted defendants' motion. Plaintiffs now appeal.

"[A] plaintiff may not recover for injuries sustained in an attack by a dog unless he or she establishes that the dog had vicious propensities and that its owner knew or should have known of such propensities'" (*Malpezzi v. Ryan,* 28 A.D.3d 1036, 1037, 815 N.Y.S.2d 295 (2006), quoting *Palleschi v. Granger,* 13 A.D.3d 871, 872, 786 N.Y.S.2d 627 (2004); *see Collier v. Zambito,* 1 N.Y.3d 444, 446, 775 N.Y.S.2d 205, 807 N.E.2d 254 (2004)). The owner's knowledge may be established by proving that the owner had notice of either a prior bite or other conduct that would give rise to an inference of vicious propensities (*see Collier v. Zambito,* 1 N.Y.3d at 446-447, 775 N.Y.S.2d 205, 807 N.E.2d 254). "[E]vidence that the dog 'had been known to growl, snap or bare its teeth' might be enough to raise a question of fact, depending on the circumstances" (*Brooks v. Parshall,* 25 A.D.3d 853, 853-854, 806 N.Y.S.2d 796 (2006), quoting *Collier v. Zambito,* 1 N.Y.3d at 447, 775 N.Y.S.2d 205, 807 N.E.2d 254). Once knowledge of a dog's vicious propensities has been established, the owner faces strict liability (*see Bard v. Jahnke,* 6 N.Y.3d 592, 596-597, 815 N.Y.S.2d 16, 848 N.E.2d 463 (2006); *Collier v. Zambito,* 1 N.Y.3d at 448, 775 N.Y.S.2d 205, 807 N.E.2d 254).

Defendants supported their motion for summary judgment with their own testimony that Sadie, whom they had owned since she was five weeks old, had never previously bitten anyone and that they had never seen her behave aggressively nor received complaints from anyone about her behavior. In addition, they submitted plaintiffs' testimony that, in numerous previous interactions with

Sadie, they had not known her to bite or threaten anyone and had never expressed concern about her to defendants (*see* CPLR 3212(b); *Rose v. Heaton,* 39 A.D.3d 937, 938, 833 N.Y.S.2d 291 (2007); *Campo v. Holland,* 32 A.D.3d 630, 631, 820 N.Y.S.2d 352 (2006); *Brooks v. Parshall,* 25 A.D.3d at 854, 806 N.Y.S.2d 796)). This evidence was sufficient to shift the burden to plaintiffs to establish the existence of triable issues of fact (*see Zuckerman v. City of New York,* 49 N.Y.2d 557, 562, 427 N.Y.S.2d 595, 404 N.E.2d 718 (1980)).

Plaintiffs' evidence was insufficient to meet their burden (*see id.*), particularly in light of their own longstanding familiarity with the dog. Plaintiffs submitted the testimony of defendants' former neighbor that Sadie barked, jumped, and ran onto the neighbor's campsite when she and her husband drove in. The campground activities director testified that on one occasion the dog frightened her by leaping off the porch, barking, and running toward her as she walked past. Neither witness had made any complaint to defendants regarding the dog's behavior. Further, these observations merely reveal "typical territorial behavior," insufficient to establish vicious propensities (*Blackstone v. Hayward,* 304 A.D.2d 941, 941-942, 757 N.Y.S.2d 160 (2003), *lv. denied* 100 N.Y.2d 511, 766 N.Y.S.2d 164, 798 N.E.2d 348 (2003); *see Campo v. Holland,* 32 A.D.3d at 631, 820 N.Y.S.2d 352; *Fontanas v. Wilson,* 300 A.D.2d 808, 808-809, 751 N.Y.S.2d 656 (2002)). Plaintiffs also submitted the testimony of plaintiff's sister and the affidavit of the sister's husband that, about a month before plaintiff was bitten, Sadie growled at the husband. A single incident of growling does not, however, establish that a dog has vicious propensities (*see Rose v. Heaton,* 39 A.D.3d at 938, 833 N.Y.S.2d 291; *Brooks v. Parshall,* 25 A.D.3d at 854, 806 N.Y.S.2d 796). Further, the husband could not confirm that either of the defendants was present during this incident, and neither he nor the sister alleged that they told defendants about it. Finally, as the campground required all dogs to be leashed, the fact that defendants kept Sadie tethered does not indicate any knowledge of the alleged vicious propensities (*see Collier v. Zambito,* 1 N.Y.3d at 447, 775 N.Y.S.2d 205, 807 N.E.2d 254). While witness testimony contradicting an owner's claims relative to a dog's conduct may be sufficient to establish issues of fact as to credibility or the owner's constructive knowledge, the proof presented here does not rise to that level (*see Loper v. Dennie,* 24 A.D.3d 1131, 1133, 807 N.Y.S.2d 672 (2005); *Czarnecki v. Welch,* 13 A.D.3d 952, 953, 786 N.Y.S.2d 659 (2004)). Defendants were therefore entitled to summary judgment dismissing the complaint.

ORDERED that the order is affirmed, with costs.

ROSE, J.P., STEIN and McCARTHY, JJ., concur.

-----------------------------------------------------------------------------------------

28 A.D.3d 1036, 815 N.Y.S.2d 295

Supreme Court, Appellate Division, Third Department, New York.
Linda MALPEZZI, Individually and as Parent and Guardian of Casey L. Malpezzi, an Infant, Respondent,
v.
Dennis RYAN, Appellant.

April 27, 2006.

CREW III, J.P.

Appeal from an order of the Supreme Court (Hoye, J.), entered June 6, 2005 in Schenectady County, which denied defendant's motion for summary judgment dismissing the complaint.

In July 2001, defendant awoke to the sound of a dog crying and discovered "Oreo" caught beneath the picnic table of his neighbor, Gerardo Masi. Defendant and Masi freed the dog and, when Oreo continued to linger on and around defendant's property, defendant contacted the local animal control officer, Rodney Hubert. According to defendant, Hubert opined that the dog, a pit bull, probably had been "dumped" because he "wasn't a fighter" and indicated that if he took the dog in, Oreo either would be claimed by someone who would try to train him to fight or he would be euthanized. As a result, defendant decided to keep Oreo and attempt to find him a home and, following Hubert's advice, contacted the local health department to ascertain whether Oreo had "a record," placed an ad in the local paper and took Oreo to a veterinarian to have him examined and vaccinated. Having received a clean bill of health from both the veterinarian and the health department, defendant took Oreo home, purchased a leash, collar and harness and set up a place for Oreo in the shed in his back yard. Over the course of the next two months, Oreo interacted with defendant, his girlfriend and their children without incident. Notably, defendant testified at his examination before trial that at no point during this time period did Oreo bark, growl or bare his teeth at, jump on or display any aggression toward any person or animal.

On the evening of September 14, 2001, defendant and his family, as was their custom, took Oreo for a walk along a local bike path where they ultimately encountered Casey Malpezzi, then six years old, and his brother, Michael. Although there is some dispute as to what then transpired, there is no question that Oreo bit Malpezzi on the arm and, as a result, plaintiff thereafter commenced this action against defendant seeking to recover for the injuries Malpezzi sustained. Following joinder of issue and discovery, defendant moved for summary judgment dismissing the complaint. Supreme Court denied that motion, finding a question of fact as to whether defendant was aware of Oreo's allegedly vicious propensities. This appeal by defendant ensued.

We reverse and grant defendant's motion for summary judgment dismissing the complaint. As this Court consistently has held, "a plaintiff may not recover for injuries sustained in an attack by a dog unless he or she establishes that the dog had vicious propensities and that its owner knew or should have known of such propensities" (*Palleschi v. Granger,* 13 A.D.3d 871, 872, 786 N.Y.S.2d 627 (2004); *see Brooks v. Parshall,* 25 A.D.3d 853, 853-854, 806 N.Y.S.2d 796 (2006); *Morse v. Colombo,* 8 A.D.3d 808, 777 N.Y.S.2d 824 (2004)). Here, defendant and his girlfriend testified, without contradiction, that they did not experience any problems with the dog prior to the incident with Malpezzi. Specifically, each testified that Oreo did not display any act of aggression prior to biting Malpezzi; Oreo did not bark, growl, bare his teeth or snap at, jump on or chase any person or animal, nor did they receive any complaints from anyone in the neighborhood. Such proof, in our view, is more than adequate to discharge defendant's initial burden on the motion for summary judgment, thereby compelling plaintiff to come forward with sufficient admissible proof to raise a question of fact in this regard. This plaintiff failed to do so.

In opposition, plaintiff primarily relies upon the purportedly vicious nature of the attack, the fact that Oreo allegedly was restrained while on defendant's property and Oreo's specific breed. As a starting point, even assuming that Oreo bit Malpezzi on the arm without provocation and in the manner alleged by plaintiff, that alone is not sufficient to raise a question of fact as to vicious propensities. Additionally, again assuming that Oreo was chained while on defendant's property-an allegation that defendant disputes-"nothing in our case law suggests that the mere fact that a dog was kept enclosed or chained ... is sufficient to raise a triable issue of fact as to whether it had vicious propensities" (*Collier v. Zambito,* 1 N.Y.3d 444, 447, 775 N.Y.S.2d 205, 807 N.E.2d 254 (2004); *see Palleschi v. Granger, supra* at 872, 786 N.Y.S.2d 627; *Hagadorn-Garmely v. Jones,* 295 A.D.2d 801, 744 N.Y.S.2d 538 (2002)). Finally, this Court repeatedly has held that "breed alone is insufficient to raise a question of fact as to vicious propensities" (*Palleschi v. Granger, supra* at 872, 786 N.Y.S.2d 627; *see Loper v. Dennie,* 24 A.D.3d 1131, 1133, 807 N.Y.S.2d 672 (2005); *Bard v. Jahnke,* 16 A.D.3d 896, 897, 791 N.Y.S.2d 694 (2005), *lv. granted* 5 N.Y.3d 708, 803 N.Y.S.2d 28, 836 N.E.2d 1151 (2005); *Mulhern v. Chai Mgt.,* 309 A.D.2d 995, 997, 765 N.Y.S.2d 694 (2003), *lv. denied* 1 N.Y.3d 508, 777 N.Y.S.2d 17, 808 N.E.2d 1276 (2004)), and we once again state that "there is no persuasive authority for the proposition that a court should take judicial notice of the ferocity of any particular type or breed of domestic animal" (*Roupp v. Conrad,* 287 A.D.2d 937, 938, 731 N.Y.S.2d 545 (2001)). Simply put, where, as here, there is no other evidence even suggesting that defendant knew or should have known of Oreo's allegedly vicious propensities, consideration of the dog's breed is irrelevant.

As such, Supreme Court erred in denying defendant's motion for summary judgment dismissing the complaint.

ORDERED that the order is reversed, on the law, with costs, motion granted, summary judgment awarded to defendant and complaint dismissed.

MUGGLIN, ROSE, LAHTINEN and KANE, JJ., concur.

*— Chapter 3 —*

# Mastering The Skill:
# How to Take Notes and Brief Cases

For a beginner law student, there is no better way to understand a case than by briefing it. A case brief is how lawyers refer to their notes on a case. When your professors and upper-class students lecture you on the importance of case briefing in law school, particularly in your first year, they are simply reminding you to take careful notes on the individual cases you read.

Keep in mind that your notes on the cases are just that—your notes. You can write in incomplete sentences, use private shorthand, highlight or bullet your text, draw pictures, etc. Essentially, you are free to use whatever style and format that works for you. Professors do not review, comment on, or grade your case briefs, unless it is part of a lesson on teaching you how to read and brief cases. Therefore, you are writing for a single audience—you. Your case briefs do not need to be helpful or even intelligible to others. Only you need to be able to understand and work with them.

Moreover, case briefs will vary greatly in content, design, and format due to differences in students' learning styles. For example, a highly verbal learner might need a lot of written text to explain the facts of a case whereas a highly visual learner might be able to explain the same facts using simple text and pictures. Therefore, you should expect to see differences between your case briefs and others. So long as those differences do not reflect a fundamental misunderstanding of the cases, they should not matter. In fact, there are no model briefs for the cases you read.

Given that case briefs are so highly individualized, copying, using, or imitating someone else's case briefs is rarely helpful and thus not recommended. It is equally unproductive to do outside research, including reading the unedited version of cases or a commercial outline's summary of them. Such research will shift your attention away from the intended purpose of the edited case toward irrelevant and distracting information. The best case briefs are ones that you create based on your reading of the opinions as edited in your casebook. They not only contain the right information, but also organize that information in a manner that is clear and accessible to you.

## The Importance of Case Briefing

Taking detailed notes on the cases you read ensures that you have more than just a superficial understanding of what happened in them. It forces you to really study a court's opinion and summarize it in a way that is useful in preparing for class, studying for exams, writing exam answers, and completing legal writing assignments. As such, the case briefing process assists you in learning how to analyze legal problems. Because analyzing legal problems is what lawyers do for a living, case briefing is not a skill practiced only in law school. Lawyers brief cases all the time so that they can learn the law in a particular area and then predict or advocate an outcome of a case for their client. Though lawyers might not brief them in the same narrative form this book teaches, their notes, whether jotted in the margins of the text or written elsewhere, capture the same information. Only after you have mastered the reading of cases and feel comfortable in your note taking skills should you attempt a less formal and more abbreviated case briefing style. Until then, and at least through the end of your first year of law school, you should prepare the type of narrative case briefs described later in this chapter.

You should also attempt to brief any notes cases that you read in the same manner. Obviously, these case briefs will be much shorter in length, as the notes cases are often boiled down to the most essential facts and a simple statement of the court's holding and reasoning. They rarely include an in-depth discussion of procedure or applicable law. Nonetheless, they are helpful in developing relevant rules and understanding those rules. Sometimes professors will surprise you and spend an entire class on a single notes case. If that happens, your brief of that notes case will help you follow the class lecture.

# The Many Purposes of a Case Brief

Case briefs serve multiple purposes. First, they promote a deep understanding of the cases you read. When briefing, you must pick out the core parts of the case and then summarize them in your notes. Also, you must figure out what rule of law applied and understand what impact that rule would likely have on a similar set of facts. Just skimming a case to a get a general idea of what happened will not give you that information. Thus, case briefing disciplines you to read carefully and pay close attention to a case's meaning and its significance on future cases.

Second, case briefs help prepare you for class discussion. In class, professors will review the cases you read to teach you important legal principles. As you now know, many will do so using the Socratic method. It can be very stressful if you are the student "on call," particularly when you did not expect it or volunteer. As discussed below, not only will your case briefs contain the answers to most of the questions your professors will ask, but the answers will also be easy to find and understand. This type of preparation will allow you to respond more competently and confidently when you are "on call". And, even when you are not "on call", case briefs will make it easier for you to follow the discussion and pick up on the relevance of any hypothetical scenarios or other questions your professors might raise. In short, they make it possible for you to stay engaged in class discussions at all times.

Third, case briefs also help you with case synthesis. As you will learn in the subsequent chapter, by looking back at your notes on previous cases, you will be able to make connections between them and see how they fit into the overall layout of a subject area. This insight is essential in helping you build a useful outline of a course—the final purpose of case briefs. The individual case briefs provide illustrations of how specific rules work. To synthesize those rules and organize them by topic, sub-topic, and so on, you will need to pull together what happened in all of the cases assigned in the course. This task would be unnecessarily complex without the aid of case briefs. Thus, case briefs are the starting point in the outlining process.

# The Parts of a Case Brief

Though case briefs are highly personal, they should all achieve the same goal. They should accurately and clearly summarize the essential parts of a case so that they can be easily used during class discussion as well as in preparation of outlining for exams. Consider using double spacing, bullet points, shading, underlining, shorthand, pictures, etc. to make them simple to read. Complete, grammatical sentences and dense text might be difficult to skim during class, particularly when you are "on call".

Heading
Facts
Procedure
Issue
Applicable Law
Holding
Rationale
Rule
Synthesis
Miscellaneous

This chapter presents the most comprehensive way to brief a case. There are sections on the core parts of a case—the relevant facts, issue, holding, and rationale—as well as the ancillary parts—the heading, procedure, and applicable law. There are also forward-looking sections on the rule and case synthesis, which are intended to prepare you for outlining, the next step in your law school journey. Finally, a miscellaneous section serves as a catch-all place for extraneous information.

Above is a list of all of the sections you might include in such a comprehensive case brief. Obviously, you should tailor the way you brief cases according to the cases themselves, your learning style, and the demands of your professors and courses. If you read and annotate cases as suggested in the previous chapter, the transition into briefing them should be smooth, as you will be relying mainly on those case annotations to write your case briefs.

In addition to explaining the sections of a case brief individually and in the order in which they appear in the brief itself, this chapter provides an illustration of each section using the *Miletich* decision from Chapter 2. These illustrations will help you see how case annotations are integrated into case briefs. The complete *Miletich* case brief can be found at the end of this chapter.

# The Heading

The heading to a case brief should contain any identifying information on the case that would be helpful in finding it later or understanding its precedential weight or historical context. At a minimum, this information should include the name of the case, the court that decided the case, the year of the decision, and the page on which it begins in the casebook. You can find most of this information in the case caption and citation.

It is not necessary to write out the entire case name in the heading; one party's name is usually sufficient to remember the case later. The court that the decided the case, which is typically next in the heading, is very illuminating because lower court and appeals court decisions are treated differently, as are federal and state court decisions. The year the case was decided is also included because it can reveal something about the political or social context of the case or the historical evolution of a legal principle.

The page on which the case appears in the casebook should be included for a practical reason. If you need to quickly turn to the case during class or at a later point when outlining, for example, you will know exactly where to go without wasting time. Information on the judge or judges who authored or participated in the decision can be included in the heading too, but only if it is noteworthy. For example, Justice Cardozo, a former United States Supreme Court Justice, wrote many landmark decisions during his eighteen-year tenure on the New York Court of Appeals. If he authored a New York decision you were assigned, you would note his name, preparing for the possibility that your professor might discuss his legal philosophy or famous prose style.

The heading for the *Miletich* case brief would look as follows:

> **Miletich**
> **New York Appellate Division, 3rd Dep't, 2010, p. 32**

# The Facts

The facts section of a case brief should summarize what happened in a case in your own words. It should include all of the relevant facts and any background facts that are necessary to tell a complete and coherent story. Remember that the relevant facts are only those that were essential to the court's decision. Facts that are neither relevant to nor helpful in understanding the decision are extraneous and should be excluded. Therefore, you should strip the facts to the bare minimum, dropping out any distracting facts, like the actual names of the parties involved, unless, of course, the names themselves are relevant to the issue. As illustrated in the facts section to the *Miletich* case brief, a description of the parties using the terms "owner" or "stranger", instead of Christopher Kopp or Heidi Miletich, respectively, is not only sufficient, but also more helpful. This simple change replaces irrelevant facts with relevant ones and makes for a clearer story.

Your case annotations on the facts is what you should use to draft this part of the brief, keeping in mind that those facts might appear in multiple places, including in the court's application of the law and reasoning. Though it might be tempting to copy verbatim the court's description of the facts, you should avoid doing so. It will be easier for you to recall the facts if you tell the story of what happened in your own words using plain English. Therefore, you should avoid using any legal jargon and quote sparingly. Only when there is language that has special significance or a particular meaning should you copy or quote it.

The facts for the *Miletich* case brief would be as follows:

- Stranger approached dog owner's door
- Dog tied nearby, sleeping
- Stranger startled dog; dog then bit her twice on leg, causing injuries
- Dog = purebred Chow Chow
- Testimony that such breed can be potentially aggressive
- Family pet since he was 8 weeks old; owned for 4 years w/o incident
- Owner routinely restrained dog to keep him from running away
- Dog was "nippy" and "territorial" when just several weeks old

Notice that this example organizes the facts in a story form, introducing the background facts before the relevant ones. It effectively employs bullet points and shorthand ("=" and "w/o") to simplify the text and make it more user-friendly. It also appropriately quotes the words "nippy" and "territorial." Because those were the exact words used to describe the dog's behavior, which was at the heart of the issue, the use of synonyms might have distorted the facts.

## The Procedure

The purpose of the procedure section of a case brief is to describe any lower court proceedings and identify the current procedural posture of the case. This information, which is also part of your case annotations, is helpful in understanding the procedural lens through which the court had to make its decision. In your first year of law school, professors like to spend a great deal of time reviewing procedure as a way to teach you the structure of the court system as well as the numerous procedural devices and motions available to litigants. This is why it is crucial that you look up any legal terms that are unfamiliar to you and include their definitions in your annotations and then case briefs.

For example, if a plaintiff appeals an order granting a defendant's motion to dismiss for failure to state a claim, you need to know what is required to state a claim properly before you can begin to understand the court's ruling on the appeal. The ruling might not finally resolve the case for the parties; it might simply decide that the plaintiff has pled sufficient facts to proceed in court. Therefore, only by knowing the procedure will you be able to properly analyze what happened in the case. As you become familiar with some of the more common procedural tools, such as motions to dismiss for failure to state a claim and motions for summary judgment, which was the motion at issue in *Miletich*, you will not need to include an explanation of them in your case briefs.

The procedure section for the *Miletich* case brief would be as follows:

- NY Supreme Ct granted D dog owner's motion for summary judgment (SJ) dismissing complaint

- Injured P (& her husband) appeals

SJ Motion = request that court decide the case (or a portion of it) without a full trial. To prevail, the moving party must establish that there are no issues of material fact requiring a trial and that in applying the law to the undisputed facts the moving party is clearly entitled to judgment in its favor.

In addition to using a simple "P" and "D" to refer to the plaintiff and defendant in the case, the example identifies their relationship to each other, as it relates to the claim at issue. This will remind you of not only what happened, but to whom. Finally, because a motion for summary judgment is a new term of art, at least as of right now, its definition is included.

# The Issue

One of the most important sections of a case brief is the statement of the issue. This section must clearly and accurately identify the question that the court analyzed. Most of the opinions you will read in law school are edited to focus on a single issue, but, in reality, most cases address more than one issue. If that is true for a case you are briefing, you will want to break up the issues (by numbers or letters, for example) so that you can address each one separately in the case brief and still be able to follow which holding, reasoning, applicable law (and maybe even relevant facts) correspond to which issue.

When the issue involves a mixed question of procedure and law, you should frame the question around the procedural posture before laying out the relevant facts, as in the *Miletich* examples that follow. Also, because questions are usually very fact-sensitive, you must be careful in how you formulate them, as a missing word or misused article can alter a question's meaning dramatically. For the *Miletich* decision, the question was not whether *any* purebred Chow Chow had vicious propensities, for example, but whether the purebred Chow Chow owned by the defendant and that had certain characteristics (family pet, owned for 4 years, etc.) had such propensities. Therefore, to be accurate, those characteristics needed to be described in the issue statement.

There are several approaches to drafting an issue statement. The *Whether. . . Where* formula is a popular and easy one to use. You begin the sentence with "Whether", then insert the core legal question, followed by a "Where" clause, which sets forth the relevant facts. Although this format is not entirely grammatical, it is an acceptable way to write issue statements in law school and after. A grammatical variation on this formula is to begin with the word "Did", then ask the core legal question followed by the word "When", which sets forth the relevant facts and ends with a question mark.

On the next page are the two ways you could state the issue for the *Miletich* decision. The substance of both issue statements is the same; the style of how the statement is presented is the only difference.

> **Whether** P demonstrated a triable issue of material fact that the purebred Chow Chow dog had vicious propensities and D owner knew or should have known of them **where** dog was family pet for 4 years since 8 weeks old and had no prior incidences of aggressiveness, but was routinely restrained to keep him from running away and was "nippy" and "territorial" when just several weeks old.
>
> **Did** P demonstrate a triable issue of material fact that the purebred Chow Chow dog had vicious propensities and D owner knew or should have known of them **when** dog was family pet for 4 years since 8 weeks old and had no prior incidences of aggressiveness, but was routinely restrained to keep him from running away and was "nippy" and "territorial" when just several weeks old?

Notice how these issue statements integrate the procedural posture of the case. If you wanted to shorten them, you could drop the introductory language "P demonstrated a triable issue of material fact that", provided that the procedural posture is included elsewhere in your case brief and you did not forget about it when referring to the issue.

Also, notice how these fact-sensitive issue statements did not include all of the relevant facts, but only the more pertinent ones, keeping them at a reasonable reading length. For example, the fact that someone testified that the breed itself might be aggressive, while relevant, was not the main basis for the court's decision. Thus, it was excluded from the issue statement, though still included in the facts section of the case brief. To do otherwise would make the issue statement too long and unwieldy.

Finally, over time, you may not need to phrase your issue statement so specific and artfully, particularly because the facts section will contain the very same facts. You might be able to state the question as simply "Whether Ds' purebred Chow Chow had vicious propensities about which they knew or should have known." Though this question would be unhelpful on its own, with practice you would know to look to the facts section for context. However, you should not truncate your issue statements like this until you are first skilled at drafting fact-specific issue statements.

# The Applicable Law

Because your annotations to a case will have isolated the law that the court used in reaching its decision on the issue before it, all of the information you will need to draft the applicable law section of the case brief will be easily accessible. The challenge is how to briefly summarize that law so that the case brief does not result in unhelpful paragraphs of dense citations to cases, statutes, secondary authorities, and other legal references. To avoid this problem, you will need to find ways to generalize or group the applicable law. This task is usually made simpler when you consider the following questions. Is the court looking to a single case or grouping of cases within its jurisdiction for guidance? Is the court looking outside its jurisdiction to persuasive authority? What types of courts decided those cases? Are they state or federal courts? Trial or appellate courts? Is there a relevant statute or constitution? Are there any references to secondary authorities like a restatement or legal treatise?

Once you have a handle on the scope of the applicable law, you can begin to categorize it so that you do not list every cited authority in the case brief. Instead, you should simply describe the law at a high level. For example, in *Miletich*, with the exception of citing one New York Court of Appeals decision, the court relied on cases by the New York Appellate Division only.[10] Therefore, the case brief for *Miletich* need only include that point. To the extent there is a particular case that is relied on more heavily or of which the facts are described, you might want to include a very brief description of it in the case brief, noting the court and year of the decision. Otherwise, it is sufficient to keep this section of the brief very general.

On the next page is the applicable law for the *Miletich* case brief:

---

[10]This information comes from the internal case citations themselves. It is evident that the decisions are New York ones based on the reporter abbreviations. The abbreviation "N.Y.S." refers to West's New York Supplement, New York's unofficial reporter, which contains decisions by all New York courts. Table 1 in the Bluebook, under New York, provides this information. There, you will also learn that the reporter abbreviation "A.D." refers to Appellate Division Reports, which contains decisions by the New York Appellate Division only. The abbreviation "N.Y." refers to New York Reports, which contains decisions by the New York Court of Appeals only. With the exception of *Collier*, which is binding authority, all of the decisions cited are of the same level court; thus, while persuasive, they have no binding effect on the *Miletich* court.

- Other than citing one New York Court of Appeals decision (*Collier*), the Court relies on New York Appellate Division cases

- *Scheidt v. Oberg* (2009) cited several times for General Rule that dog owner is liable for injuries caused by his or her dog when the dog has vicious propensities and the owner knew or should have known of such propensities

- Specific Rule for <u>vicious propensities</u>: may include evidence of prior vicious behavior such as biting, growling, snapping or baring its teeth; breed alone not sufficient, though may be considered w/ other factors

- Specific Rule for <u>knowledge of propensities</u>: may include evidence that dog used as guard dog or owner restrained it out of concern that dog will put others at risk of harm

You should immediately notice how this section is organized into general and specific rules. The rules correspond to the legal principles. The general rule is obviously the most general legal principle. As the court expands and explains how a plaintiff can satisfy that general rule, you learn more details about the law, which is why that information is referred to as a specific rule. It is advisable for you to adopt this same terminology so that you too can organize the law on any given topic from the general to the specific.

## The Holding

This section briefly states the court's resolution of the issue. It does not address the court's reasoning, however, because the next section of the case brief does just that. No discussion on this section would be complete without mentioning the word *dictum* (the plural for the Latin term is *dicta*)—a concept you should learn, but not obsess over. Simply stated, when a judge expresses an opinion on how the law would apply to a set of facts not before it that judge's opinion will not be binding in subsequent cases as legal precedent. Because the judge's views were unnecessary in resolving the parties' dispute, they were irrelevant to the court's decision. As such, they are dicta and not part of the court's holding.

However, just because dictum is irrelevant and not binding on future courts does not mean that it has no value whatsoever. Dictum is usually very informative and helpful in explaining the contours of a court's decision. In fact, a court might purposefully include dictum to explain or support its decision. For example, if the *Miletich* court wrote in its reasoning: "Had there been evidence that the dog was "nippy" and "territorial" *in recent months*, there would be a triable issue of fact," that general pronouncement would be dictum—and you would annotate it as such. That dictum would give us some insight into the court's thinking, however. It is not that being "nippy" or "territorial" are never sufficient to raise a triable issue of fact, it is how recently the dog exhibited that behavior that is important. It is dictum, though, because the facts—in recent months—were not actually before the *Miletich* court.

Dictum also has another use. It can be a signal for how a court might resolve a future case. In fact, in practice when there is no or only weak legally binding precedent, lawyers will use dictum as persuasive authority for why the law should be applied in the way they advocate. Therefore, you should not ignore it. And, although it is not part of a court's holding, and should not be described as such, there is a place for it in a case brief. You can either include it in the reasoning section if it helps explain the court's decision or in the miscellaneous section described later.

Dictum is easy to spot when courts use "If" clauses; but not every decision has dictum. In fact, most decisions do not. Therefore, you should not waste time searching for it. Rather, spend your time deciding whether what the court said and did was necessary to resolving the parties' dispute. If the answer is yes, there is no dictum.

For the holding itself, simply answer the issue statement, by giving a short answer first, followed by a more detailed one. The holding for the *Miletich* case brief would be as follows:

No. There is no evidence that the dog had vicious propensities or that the defendant owner knew or should have known of such propensities.

## The Rationale

Because the holding alone is insufficient to explain the court's resolution of the issue, the rationale section of the case brief summarizes why the court ruled the way it did. When the court is answering a legal question that is fact-specific, this section will often overlap with your Facts, Holding, and Applicable Law sections. Try not to get so caught up in deciding under which section the information should go; the most important thing is that the case brief captures all of the key information. If some of the court's reasoning is in the Holding section or applicable law in the Rationale section, for example, it does not matter. They are all linked.

The reasoning for the *Miletich* decision is one such example where the reasoning is essentially a restatement of how the facts were not sufficient to raise a triable issue on vicious propensities or knowledge of such propensities. Thus, the distinction between the Facts, Holding, and Rationale sections is negligible here.

- Evidence that owners restrained dog did not support inference that owners were aware that dog might pose a danger
- Evidence that dog was "nippy" or "territorial" when he was young similarly did not raise triable issue of fact
- Testimony that the Chow Chow breed are potentially aggressive and there are incidences of aggressiveness involving that breed does not, by itself, create an issue of fact regarding vicious propensities in D's dog
- Manner in which P was bitten also does not support inference that dog was aggressive b/c P never saw dog until immediately before she was bitten and dog was startled from his sleep
- Family pet for 4 years—Ds not aware of any incidences prior to one in dispute

# The Rule

This section of the case brief does not have a direct corollary in your annotations to the case. This is where you will begin thinking about what impact the case will have on future cases with similar facts. Because your end goal is to be able to analyze problems on the same issue, you must move beyond the specific facts of the case and develop notes that help you in this regard. Essentially, you must ask: What rule (legal principle) can be distilled from the case? That rule will become part of your course outline and will be used to answer exam questions on the same issue. Thus, in order for the rule to be useful, it must be stated general enough to apply to cases with similar facts. In other words, it must not be stated narrowly or be so fact-specific that it only applies to the case you briefed.

Moreover, there might be more than one rule that comes out of a case. This is true for the *Miletich* decision. Even though the issue was framed as a single question, there were really two parts to answering that question. The first was whether there was sufficient evidence that the dog had vicious propensities and the second was whether there was sufficient evidence that the owner knew of or should have known of those propensities. Therefore, the *Miletich* decision produced two rules that will influence future cases. They are as follows:

Specific Rules on Vicious Propensities:
1.  Evidence that a dog was "nippy" or "territorial" when he was young does not demonstrate that a dog has vicious propensities when that dog has no incidences during the rest of its life.
2.  The manner in which a plaintiff was injured is relevant in deciding whether a dog has vicious propensities. For example, evidence that a dog injured a stranger after being startled by that stranger (i.e., woken from sleep) does not suggest an aggressive dog.

Specific Rules on Knowledge:
1.  Evidence that a dog owner restrains a dog to keep it from running away (not out of concern that dog will harm others) does not demonstrate that owner knew or should have known that the dog had vicious propensities.
2.  Evidence that a dog's breed is potentially aggressive and there are incidences of aggressiveness involving that breed does not, by itself, demonstrate that owner knew or should have known that the dog had vicious propensities.

These specific rules expand or further develop the existing applicable law that the court relied on in reaching its decision. Moreover, they are helpful in deciding the next case in which a dog injures a person, one that raises the same issue but involves a set of facts different from those in *Miletich*. The existence or nonexistence of the factors outlined above will assist in predicting how a court will likely resolve that case. Therefore, the Rule section is an important step in building your course outline and preparing for exam questions.

## The Synthesis Section

Like the Rule section, the Synthesis section has no counterpart in your case annotations and also serves a forward-looking purpose. This is where you will examine the case in relation to other cases or material you have read on the topic and draw connections between them. You should consider whether the case establishes a general rule on the issue, explains a rule (i.e. develops a specific rule), carves out an exception to a rule, or changes or overturns a prevailing rule. Importantly, you are thinking about why the professor asked you to read the case. Why is the case important? How does it fit into the course outline? Is there any dictum? What impact does it have on future cases?

These are the types of questions you should consider as you synthesize the material. The important lesson here is that you are looking at the case in relation to the entire course. Referring to the casebook's table of contents or the course syllabus will help you make the appropriate connections in the material. This section usually evolves as you complete your reading on a specific topic or chapter.

For the *Miletich* decision, if the professor assigned it along with the *Illian* and *Malpezzi* cases, you would quickly see that together they explain the factors courts consider and the weight they are given in deciding whether a dog owner is strictly liable for injuries his or her dog causes. The *Miletich* decision is later in time, but still consistent with the earlier decisions. Here's what your Synthesis section might look like for *Miletich*, assuming that you already read and briefed the two other decisions:

---

Consistent with Illian/Ryan decisions.

Factors in deciding vicious propensities (no one factor on its own is sufficient):
- Evidence that dog barks, growls, bares teeth, jumps on or runs after passersby or cars, or acts aggressive; however, single instance of any such behavior or evidence that dog is "territorial" is not enough
- Manner in which plaintiff was injured
- Evidence that dog's breed is aggressive
- Evidence that dog was restrained

---

Factors in deciding knowledge:
- Evidence that dog owner restrains dog relevant, but reason matters. Is dog restrained b/c it acts aggressively?
- Evidence that dog's breed is aggressive relevant, but by itself, is not dispositive.
- Evidence that dog owner received complaints about dog's aggressive behavior
- Evidence that dog owner had notice of prior bite or other aggressive conduct

# The Miscellaneous Section

In this section of the case brief, you can put any extraneous information or tidbits from the case that are interesting, but do not apply to the other sections. Among that information is the disposition of the case, which is the entire substance of the miscellaneous section in the *Miletich* case brief. It is as follows:

The complaint was properly dismissed.

The Court affirmed the lower court's decision.

It could also include an explanation of dictum and summaries of any concurring or dissenting opinions. Even though dissenting or concurring opinions, like dictum, are not binding authority, oftentimes they will help you understand, among other things, the boundaries of the rule from the case, the majority court's reasoning, and the development of the law over time (especially in cases where the dissent later becomes the majority opinion). If these types of opinions were not edited out of your casebooks, they were intended to teach you something about the relevant legal principles. That something should be addressed in this section.

This is also an appropriate place for you to define legal terms of art or procedure that you decoded in your reading of the case and annotated as a way to build your legal vocabulary and learn new procedure. Finally, this section is a good place to jot down any questions or concerns that you have about the case or its relationship to other cases. You will want to keep a record of your questions or concerns contemporaneous with your briefing of the cases so that you do not forget them.

Therefore, this section usually contains a wide array of personal and other miscellaneous information.

## Beyond the Case Brief: Notetaking During and After Class

Your case briefs are the foundation for the notes that you will take during class. You will mostly be editing or adding new information to them. Therefore, it is essential that you have either a hard copy or electronic version of them in class with you. If you are using an electronic version, you should save the case brief as a new document so that you do not erase your original notes on the case. Sometimes those notes are useful in clearing up questions you might have had about the case or what was discussed in class.

You will want to focus on several key areas when modifying your case briefs during class. First, you should note any discrepancies between what you summarized and what was addressed by the professor. Second, you should add any new information; this includes information you either missed or was raised for the first time in class. Third, you should check off what you summarized correctly so that you are not left guessing as to the accuracy of your case briefs at a later point in time.

Fourth, you should add any new questions or concerns that you have but were unable to resolve during class. If you were confused in class, you should assume that you will be confused later as well. In order to stay engaged in the material, you will want an opportunity to resolve any confusion you have. Because the pace of a law school class is fast, you might not remember until exam time that you did not fully understand a topic. Taking immediate notes on the questions you have will ensure that you do not forget to get answers to them.

Fifth, you should write down any hypothetical scenarios or new fact patterns that were discussed. These are great illustrations of how courts resolve problems on the same issue and thus will help your understanding of the relevant rules. Finally, if the professor mentions a term with which you are unfamiliar, write it down and look it up after class. If the professor defines a term of art, you should make note of its meaning too. These types of notations will help you improve your legal vocabulary and master procedural law.

As you modify your case briefs, try your best to make changes in the appropriate sections, rather than just jotting down notes anywhere, as this will only create more work for you later. Though taking notes on your computer might allow you to take dictation of a professor's lecture as well as the entire Socratic dialogue, avoid the temptation to do so. Instead, carefully listen to the discussion and process how it relates to your notes on the case. Only after filtering irrelevant and erroneous information should you write anything down. As mentioned earlier, if you are able to do so, attempt to place that information in its appropriate place in the case brief immediately. Good note takers listen to what is said, digest its meaning, and then record the material parts of it in a way that is connected to their case briefs. Moreover, pay careful attention to how professors introduce or conclude their lecture on a case; oftentimes they present great clues on a relationship one case has to another or the overall course—information essential to your synthesis of the material.

Your note taking does not end when class is over. Soon after class, and certainly before your reading for the next class, you should review your edited case briefs and other notes. You should use this time as an opportunity to clean up the rushed, shorthand notes that you took in class. If you were unable to place the information in the right place during class, you should do so after class. If you had questions, try to answer them as well. If you cannot answer them on your own, work with a study group or the professor to resolve them.

Finally, revise your rule and synthesis sections to incorporate any discussions about how the law developed from one case to another. Once you have completed a chapter or topic, you should review these sections again to get a more complete and accurate layout of the law. As mentioned earlier, this section will continually evolve. The importance of cases and how they fit together does not always become apparent until the end of a chapter or topic. Regardless of when it happens, case synthesis is the vital link between case briefing and outlining—the next step in the process and the subject of the following chapter.

## Sample Miletich Case Brief

## MILETICH

New York Appellate Division, 3d Dep't

2010

p. 32

**Facts:**

- Stranger approached dog owner's door
- Dog tied nearby, sleeping
- Stranger startled him; he then bit her twice on leg, causing injuries
- Dog = purebred Chow Chow
- Testimony that such breed can be potentially aggressive
- Family pet since he was 8 weeks old; owned for 4 years w/o incident
- Owner routinely restrained dog to keep him from running away
- Dog was "nippy" and "territorial" when just several weeks old

**Procedure:**

- NY Supreme Ct granted D dog owner's motion for summary judgment (SJ) dismissing complaint

- Injured P (& her husband) appeals

SJ Motion = request that court decide the case (or a portion of it) without a full trial. To prevail, the moving party must establish that there are no issues of material fact requiring a trial and that in applying the law to the undisputed facts the moving party is clearly entitled to judgment in its favor.

**Issue:**

Whether P demonstrated a triable issue of material fact that the purebred Chow Chow dog had vicious propensities and D owner knew or should have known of them where dog was family pet for 4 years since 8 weeks old and had no prior incidences of aggressiveness, but was routinely restrained to keep him from running away and was "nippy" and "territorial" when just several weeks old.

**Applicable Law:**

- Other than citing one New York Court of Appeals decision (*Collier*), the Court relies on New York Appellate Division cases

- *Scheidt v. Oberg* (2009) cited several times for General Rule that dog owner is liable for injuries caused by his or her dog when the dog has vicious propensities and the owner knew or should have known of such propensities

- Specific Rule for <u>vicious propensities</u>: may include evidence of prior vicious behavior such as biting, growling, snapping or baring its teeth; breed alone not sufficient, though may be considered w/ other factors

- Specific Rule for <u>knowledge of propensities</u>: may include evidence that dog used as guard dog or owner restrained it out of concern that dog will put others at risk of harm

**Holding:**

No. There is insufficient evidence that the dog had vicious propensities or that the defendant owner knew or should have known of such propensities.

**Rationale:**

- Evidence that owners restrained dog did not support inference that owners were aware that dog might pose a danger

- Evidence that dog was "nippy" or "territorial" when he was young similarly did not raise triable issue of fact

- Testimony that the Chow Chow breed are potentially aggressive and there are incidences of aggressiveness involving that breed does not, by itself, create an issue of fact regarding vicious propensities in D's dog

- Manner in which P was bitten also does not support inference that dog was aggressive b/c P never saw dog until immediately before she was bitten and dog was startled from his sleep

- Family pet for 4 years—Ds not aware of any incidences prior to one in dispute

**Rule:**

Specific Rules on Vicious Propensities:
1. Evidence that a dog was "nippy" or "territorial" when he was young does not demonstrate that a dog has vicious propensities when that dog has no incidences during the rest of its life.
2. The manner in which a plaintiff was injured is relevant in deciding whether a dog has vicious propensities. For example, evidence that a dog injured a stranger after being startled by that stranger (i.e., woken from sleep) does not suggest an aggressive dog.

Specific Rules on Knowledge:

1. Evidence that a dog owner restrains a dog to keep it from running away (not out of concern that dog will harm others) does not demonstrate that owner knew or should have known that the dog had vicious propensities.

2. Evidence that a dog's breed is potentially aggressive and there are incidences of aggressiveness involving that breed does not, by itself, demonstrate that owner knew or should have known that the dog had vicious propensities.

**Synthesis:**

Consistent with Illian/Malpezzi decisions.

Factors in deciding vicious propensities (no one factor on its own is sufficient):

- Evidence that dog barks, growls, bares teeth, jumps on or runs after passersby or cars, or acts aggressive; however, single instance of any such behavior or evidence that dog is "territorial" is not enough
- Manner in which plaintiff was injured
- Evidence that dog's breed is aggressive
- Evidence that dog was restrained

Factors in deciding knowledge:

- Evidence that dog owner restrains dog relevant, but reason matters. Is dog restrained b/c it acts aggressively?
- Evidence that dog's breed is aggressive relevant, but by itself, is not dispositive.
- Evidence that dog owner received complaints about dog's aggressive behavior
- Evidence that dog owner had notice of prior bite or other aggressive conduct

**Misc.:**

The complaint was properly dismissed.  The Court affirmed the lower court's decision.

# Chapter 3 Exercise:

Prepare case briefs for the two cases at the end of Chapter 2—the *Illian* and *Malpezzi* decisions.

# — *Chapter 4* —

# Constructing an Outline of a Course

Your outline of a course is the key to successfully preparing and studying for exams. This single document compiles all of the legal rules covered in a course and illustrates how those rules play out in various factual scenarios. It is rooted in the work you did throughout the semester. In fact, most of the outline stems directly from your case briefs and class notes. The rules are the legal principles that you synthesized from the cases or developed from the statutes, constitutions, and other legal authority you studied. The illustrations or, more accurately, the rule applications, include what happened in the cases you briefed and hypotheticals you discussed. The outline also contains whatever other information you took notes on or briefed that helps to explain the rules and rule applications; this information might include, among other things, definitions of legal terms of art, reasoning, policy discussions, historical background, and counterarguments.

An effective outline is more than just comprehensive, though. The text is usually succinct and clear. It is easy to follow too. The material is organized logically by topic with the information moving from the most general to the most specific. In this way, it serves as a roadmap or written instructions on how to analyze and solve legal questions on any topic addressed in the course. In other words, once complete, it teaches you how to answer potential exam questions.

However, the real benefit of an outline comes from creating one. The process of organizing the material into helpful instructions virtually guarantees that you will learn the law and how to apply it appropriately. Just like you should write your own case briefs, you should write your own outlines, and not rely on other students' outlines or commercial ones. If you use a prepared outline, you will spend disproportionately more time memorizing the doctrine as arranged by the outline's author than interacting with and studying the material your professor emphasized in class and wanted you to learn.

Moreover, you will pass over the writing process entirely—an indispensable part of your learning the law. The writing process itself is what forces you to review your course material, synthesize the law, and then organize what you learned into a coherent structure. It is through this process that your grasp of the law and its application to other cases is usually cemented. When you use another's outline exclusively, this step in your studying does not occur. As a result, you miss out on an important opportunity to improve your knowledge of the law and consequently your performance on exams.

This is not to say that prepared outlines have no utility. Some students consult them for ideas on organization or to clarify the law, especially when dealing with complex concepts. Others find it helpful to compare their work against prepared outlines to check their progress or confirm they are on the right track. It can be reassuring to see that your presentation and development of the material is similar to another's. Remember, however, that prepared outlines are not a substitute for doing your own. They are not tailored to how your professor taught the course and what he or she expects from you on the exam. Therefore, you should be careful not to give too much weight to what you learn from them.

For better guidance, you should meet with your professors, or any teaching assistants, and form study groups with your classmates. Study groups are a great resource. Among other things, you can use them to discuss how to organize the law and best explain the relevant rules and rule applications. Even if you decide to work alone, it is your professor's expectations, not someone else's, that should drive how you build your outline of a course.

## Outlining is Not a Foreign Activity

It will be easier for you to tackle outlining if you can see that the process is similar to a non-legal activity you have probably done before: organizing a wardrobe. Imagine that you cleared out your closet as part of a spring cleaning frenzy. You dumped all of your clothing into a big pile on the floor. In this disorganized state, the only thing obviously similar about the items in the pile is that they are all articles of clothing. To organize your closet, you would need to sort through the clothes and divide them into more manageable piles by type of clothing.

For instance, there might be a pile of shirts, sweaters, shorts, pants, and jackets. You would then need to work on each of these piles individually, creating even smaller ones sorted by sub-type and then color. If you were to start with the shirt pile, you would probably subdivide it into casual and dress ones; within each of those piles you would then separate the white shirts from the colored ones and patterned ones. You would sort all of the clothing this way, making as many smaller piles as both feasible and practical. All along the goal would be to create an organization that would allow you to find whatever clothes you wanted to wear fast and effortlessly.

Similarly, the goal of outlining is to lay out the course material into a usable format so that you can easily and quickly find the answer to any legal problem on a single subject matter. Instead of clothes, you must sift through the judicial opinions, your annotations and case briefs of those opinions, class notes, and anything else you covered over the course of the semester. At the beginning of the process, the material might seem just as disorganized as the pile of clothes cleared from the closet and tossed on the floor. Though all of the material will relate to the same doctrine, it will need to be arranged into smaller parts by topics, sub-topics, sub-subtopics and so on, just like the different types of clothing in your closet. Hence, the process of organizing a course into an outline will be a familiar one.

## Building Your Outline

The first step of outlining is to lay out the main topics and sub-topics of the course. In doing so, you should use your course syllabus, the casebook table of contents, and any class notes that give you an overview of the course. For example, if you were outlining your Torts class, there would be separate headings on your syllabus and in the casebook table of contents devoted to the three main types of torts: intentional acts, negligence, and strict liability. Therefore, these main topics would form separate categories in your outline.

**Torts Outline**

- Intentional Acts
  - Assault
  - Battery

- Negligence

- Strict Liability

Additionally, they would be placed on "equal footing," as depicted in the earlier diagram, because each type of tort is distinct from the other and has its own sub-topics. For instance, there are several different types of intentional acts, among them assault and battery. These two sub-topics, as illustrated, also would be on "equal footing" in the outline for the same reasons as the main topics.

After you have established the skeletal structure of the outline, the next step is to begin filling in the details. You will start by inserting the general rules for the main topics and sub-topics. Those rules might involve elements that a party must prove to prevail on an issue or factors that courts balance in deciding an issue. In either case, there is usually an opportunity to break down the outline even more by element or factor. You would then add the specific rules for the individual elements or factors next. If there were exceptions to a rule or a majority and minority rule on a single issue, you would include them too.

In the Torts outline to the right, some of the details for the sub-topic battery have been added. The definition, which is signaled by "=", is presented before any of its sub-parts. That definition is the general rule for battery. The general rule is then broken down into its elements with each element having its own entry. For now, the offensive element is the only element explained further. The statement after the "=" sign is the specific rule for what constitutes offensive contact.

Before moving on, you should notice how the outline effectively makes use of bulleting, indenting, and symbols. Each different topic has its own bullet point. Moreover, the bullet points and corresponding text are indented every time a

**Torts Outline**

- Intentional Acts
  - Assault
  - Battery= Actor intended to cause a contact that is harmful or offensive.
    - o Intent
    - &
    - o Contact
    - &
    - o Harmful
    - or
    - o Offensive=contact that is offensive to a reasonable sense of personal dignity (objective test)

- Negligence

- Strict Liability

topic is examined in greater depth. This format nicely parallels the outline's movement from general rules to specific ones, making it simple to follow. Through the use of the "&" symbol and the word "or" in all caps, the outline also makes clear that not all of the listed elements are required to establish a battery. Thus, it is unambiguous that the contact may be either harmful or offensive to establish a battery; it need not be both.

If you were to continue developing this outline, all of the elements would be expanded eventually, but only to the fullest extent allowable by your case annotations and briefs, notes, and other materials. Again, you would use only the material you were given. You would not attempt to fill in missing information using outside resources. If your professor never taught or assigned the information, he or she will not expect you to know it for the exam. Thus, it is all right if the amount of content in your outline varies greatly from one entry to another, as is the case in the sub-topic Battery in the more complete Torts outline beginning on the following page.

Once the outline contains all of the general and specific rules, it is time to plug in the rule applications—that is, examples of how those rules are applied. The examples will emanate from the main cases, notes cases, hypotheticals, and any other cases you discussed. Importantly, the cases and related hypotheticals—which were the main focus of your note taking and case briefing—will not be the focal point of the outline. Rather, the spotlight will be on the general and specific rules—the ones you synthesized in your case briefs. The cases and hypotheticals will now serve as examples of how those rules work. Moreover, case names will be relegated to parentheticals at the end of the case explanations. Unless a case is well-known or your professor expects you to use case names in explaining a rule, the case names are no longer important.

Returning to the Torts outline from earlier, the example on the next page shows what the outline would look like when the sub-topic Battery is completely outlined. The other three elements—intent, contact, and harmful—now have been expanded to include their specific rules and rule applications. The specific rule for the offensive element has been elaborated on as well. There are also rule applications—examples of contact that is and is not offensive. Implicit in their subheadings *Offensive* and *Not Offensive* are the holdings of the cases and outcomes of the hypotheticals listed. The relevant facts from those cases and hypotheticals are stated succinctly after these headings. Because the same reasoning applied in all of the *offensive* as well as *not offensive* examples, a single bullet point under each heading is sufficient. There was only one policy argument in this example and it further explained why the cellular phone and bubblegum scenarios were not offensive, which is why it appears after the reasoning bullet point for that heading. This type of policy argument and any social, economic, political or governmental concerns that likewise explain a rule or rule application are usually included at the end, as is the case here.

---

**Torts Outline**

- Intentional Acts
  - Assault
  - Battery= Actor intended to cause a contact that is harmful or offensive.
    - Intent
      - Single Intent Rule: Defendant need only intend contact, not that it be harmful or offensive
        - Example: D intended to tap knee, not to cause harm (practical joke) but still liable (Case A) AND
    - Contact=touching someone's person or touching something closely connected with the person's body
      - Examples: touching someone's clothing; knocking hat off someone's head; knocking glass out of someone's hand (all hypos) AND
    - Harmful=physical harm (i.e., cut, scrape, gunshot wound) OR
    - Offensive=contact that is offensive to a reasonable sense of personal dignity (objective test)
      - Offensiveness includes "disagreeable or nauseating or painful because of outrage to taste and sensibilities or affronting insultingness"
        - Offensive: Tapping knee (Case A); blowing smoke in face (Case B); bug spray (hypo)
          - Reasoning: Conduct would offend an average person in society; unpleasant physical contact and smell
        - Not Offensive: talking loudly on cellular phone in doctor's office (hypo); snapping bubblegum on

---

airplane (hypo)
- o  Reasoning:  Conduct would not offend average person in society; while annoying, not unpleasant to sense of hearing
- o  Policy:  Too many people use cell phones & chew gum to begin restricting behavior; also enforcement would be impractical

- Negligence

- Strict Liability

One final way to conceptualize the outline is to think of it as an expandable tree. Thus, if the example Torts outline were online, the outline would be the tree and each bullet point would be a branch.  You would be able to click on every branch of the tree to expand the information under that bullet point.  With each click through of the tree's branches, the information would become more specific until there were no more branches to expand.  Similarly, you should click through or expand on every topic of your outline until there is no more information remaining in your case briefs or class notes.  The visual of an expandable tree is a good way to remember that outlining requires you to assemble all that you learned in a course into a format that efficiently displays the law and its application to different factual scenarios.

Now that you know what an outline encompasses, it should be patently obvious as to why case briefing is such a crucial part of creating an effective outline.  You will rely heavily on your edited case briefs and class notes to build all parts of the outline.  Specifically, you will use the Issue, Rule, Applicable Law, and Synthesis sections of the case briefs to help define the overall structure of the outline, including the main topics and sub-topics.  Additionally, you will pull from the Facts, Holding, and Reasoning sections of the case briefs to draft the rule applications. Basically, everything you need to build an outline can be found in your case briefs.

Because the outline will serve as your study aid for exams, it should be organized in a way that works for you.  Just like your case briefs and class notes might look different than your classmates', so too might your outlines.  They should reflect your system of organization and learning style.  Therefore, you should not try to adopt a format that is counterintuitive to you. If indenting and using bullet points is not a good visual for you, consider other methods of organization, such as color coding, flow charts, numbering, etc. As long as your outline is complete and follows a hierarchical structure, moving from the general to the specific, the presentation itself does not really matter. What matters is that you can use it effectively to study and prepare for exams.

## Using the Outline to Prepare for Exams

The advantage of making your own outline is that the end result is a personalized study guide. Your outline has all of the rules and rule applications that your professor would expect you to know on an exam. Moreover, the rule applications teach you how to appropriately apply those rules in circumstances like the ones on your exam. For all intents and purposes, your outline provides detailed instructions on how to approach and answer any exam question on the topics covered in the course. Therefore, you will want to memorize those instructions. You will want to learn the rules and internalize how they apply in practice so that you can recall both at exam time.

The best way to memorize and internalize the material is to continually review your outline. Once you become comfortable with most of the material or chunks of it, you can begin to collapse the outline. In contrast to the expanding you did to build the outline, you would collapse the branches of the tree you know well until you are left with only the most general branches of it. If you need a visual, look at the examples of the Torts outline from earlier in this chapter again, except now in reverse. You will know when you have mastered all of the material when you are able to collapse the outline into a single page listing of the main topics and sub-topics only.

This collapsed outline will remind you of the issues you should be "spotting" on the exam as well as test your knowledge of the rules and rule applications. Because first-year law students are usually prohibited from using their outlines on exams, you need to be able to look at a topic heading and immediately recall all of the information that flows from it. Use the collapsed outline to aid in this process.

The more you are able to shrink the outline, the closer you are to completing your studying.

## Using the Outline to Answer Exam Questions

Now that you know how to prepare a course outline, it is time to see how you can use that outline to analyze legal problems. Indeed, a useful outline should be able to guide you through the many issues that arise on a subject and provide step-by-step instructions on how to resolve some of the more common factual scenarios. To illustrate the connection between the course outline and an exam problem, we will revisit the sample client problem from Chapter 1 using the *Miletich, Illian,* and *Malpezzi* decisions from Chapter 2. If you were to outline the law relating to a dog owner's liability for injuries caused by his or her dog, you would end up with a draft similar to the one on the next page.

# TORTS OUTLINE

1. Intentional Acts

2. Negligence

3. Strict Liability

- An Owner's Liability for Injuries Caused by a Pet

  - Dogs: Owner is strictly liable for injuries when the dog has vicious propensities and the owner should have known or knew of such propensities. (*Collier*)

    - Vicious Propensities: the following evidence is relevant in deciding vicious propensities; none of the evidence on its own is sufficient
      - Evidence that dog often barks, growls, bares teeth, jumps on or runs after passersby or cars, or otherwise acts aggressive; a single instance of a dog growling is not sufficient. (*Illian*)
        - Example: Evidence that a dog barks, jumps, or runs after passersby or cars is insufficient to raise a triable issue of fact in the absence of any other evidence of aggressive behavior by the dog. (*Illian*)
        - Example: Evidence that a dog was "nippy" or "territorial" when he was young does not demonstrate that a dog has vicious propensities when that dog has no incidences during the rest of its life. (*Miletich*)
      - Manner in which plaintiff was injured
        - Example: Evidence that a dog injured a stranger after being startled by that stranger (i.e., woken from sleep) does not suggest an aggressive dog. (*Miletich*)
      - Evidence that dog's breed is aggressive
        - Example: no vicious propensities where pit bull bit 6 yr old boy w/o provocation b/c no evidence suggesting dog was vicious other than breed is known to be (*Malpezzi*)
      - Evidence that dog was restrained

    - Knowledge: the following evidence is relevant in deciding an owner's knowledge; none of the evidence on its own is sufficient
      - Evidence that dog owner restrains dog, but reason matters.

Is dog restrained b/c it acts aggressively?
- Example: Evidence that a dog owner restrains a dog because a rule requires that owner to do so does not prove knowledge of vicious propensities. (*Illian*)
- Example: Evidence that a dog owner restrains a dog to keep it from running away (not out of concern that dog will harm others) does not prove knowledge of vicious propensities. (*Miletich*)

- Evidence that dog's breed is aggressive
- Evidence that dog owner received complaints about dog's aggressive behavior
- Evidence that dog owner had notice of prior bite or other aggressive conduct

Obviously, this draft would be part of a larger outline on the subject of Torts. An owner's liability for injuries caused by his or her dog would be just one sub-topic covered in the course under the topic Strict Liability using the *Miletich*, *Illian* and *Malpezzi* cases. As explained in the previous chapter, when it comes time to outline, the cases themselves become subordinate to the law that was synthesized from them; for that reason, in this example outline, the general and specific rules of law are outlined first, followed by the facts and reasoning of the cases—examples of those rules.

Returning to the sample problem, if you recall, the client, Mr. Gerardi, wanted to know whether he was liable for injuries his dog, a Golden Retriever, caused to a young boy while he was walking his dog without a leash in a public park. The rest of the client's story is repeated here for your reference.

The boy was playing on the sidewalk, unaware of the dog, until the attack. The boy sought medical attention from a local hospital's emergency room. His parents have sent Mr. Gerardi the hospital bill along with a demand for reimbursement. According to Mr. Gerardi, his dog is gentle; however, there was one prior incident in which the dog scratched a stranger. The dog was similarly unleashed. The stranger required no medical attention.

The example outline tells us that this problem raises two issues: (1) whether Mr. Gerardi's dog has vicious propensities and (2) whether Mr. Gerardi had knowledge of such propensities. For the first issue, the relevant factors include the dog's past and present behavior, the manner in which the boy was injured, the dog's breed, and whether it was ever restrained. Other than a single scratching incident, which is not uncommon for a typical dog, there is no evidence that the dog acted aggressively with any frequency or was ever restrained out of concern that it would do harm. There is no evidence of barking, growling, or baring its teeth, for example. Moreover, the dog's breed—a Golden Retriever—is not known to be aggressive. Rather, Golden Retrievers are known to be devoted, obedient, loving family dogs. In fact, Mr. Gerardi describes him as "gentle." Though the dog was unprovoked when it injured the boy, like in *Malpezzi*, absent any other evidence of the dog's viciousness, this factor alone is insufficient to establish vicious propensities. Accordingly, the first issue is resolved in Mr. Gerardi's favor and, as such, absolves him of any liability.

Even so, for completeness, you still would analyze the second issue. There is also no evidence that Mr. Gerardi had knowledge of any vicious propensities, as none of the relevant factors are present. There is no evidence that he restrained the dog for any reason, received complaints about the dog's behavior, or had notice of a prior bite or other aggressive conduct. Moreover, the Golden Retriever breed is not aggressive in any way. Therefore, because the child will be unable to establish either element, Mr. Gerardi will not be strictly liable for his injuries.

Through this example, you can see how easy it is to move from the broad question posed by the client to the legal issues that you have to analyze in order to answer the client's question. Because the outline explicitly lays out the issues that are associated with a question like Mr. Gerardi's, you can quickly spot them. The rules for each of the issues are also handy, making it simple for you to apply them to your client's facts and quickly reach a conclusion on the client's question. Thus, the outline is your roadmap to answering any legal problem your professor might give you on an exam. Accordingly, its value cannot be emphasized enough.

# Chapter 4 Exercise:

Assume you are working on the Torts outline illustrated in this chapter. Now that the sub-topic Battery is complete, you must begin working on the sub-topic Assault. The following information comes from your case briefs and class notes, but is currently unorganized. Rearrange the information from the general to the specific using whatever format and presentation style that works for you.

a. There are two types of intent that will satisfy this tort: specific and general intent. Either one is sufficient.

b. An example of a threat that would not be immediate is a threat to kill a person 5 years from now.

c. The actor must produce apprehension in the mind of a reasonable person. Whether there is *apprehension* will depend on the circumstances. For example, it might take less time to create apprehension in the mind of a child than an adult.

d. While battery requires a harmful or offensive contact, assault merely requires apprehension that a harmful or offensive contact is about to occur.

e. Specific intent occurs when the actor intends to cause the apprehension of harmful or offensive contact in the victim.

f. In *Case D*, the court held that Plaintiff did not have reasonable apprehension of a harmful contact when he was sleeping at the time that Defendant clenched his fist to throw a punch at him.

g. Assault occurs when the actor intended to put someone in apprehension of an immediate harmful or offensive contact.

h. General intent occurs when the actor intends to do the act that causes such apprehension, even if the actor did not intend to cause apprehension in the victim himself or herself.

i. In *Case C*, the court held that Plaintiff had reasonable apprehension of a harmful contact when Defendant threw a rock at her, but missed.

j. In *Case A*, Defendant intended to swing his arm at Plaintiff. Therefore, the court held that Defendant had specific intent to put Plaintiff in apprehension of an immediate harmful contact.

k. In a hypothetical, we discussed how a person would likely not have a reasonable apprehension of harmful or offensive contact when someone else blows bubbles in his or her direction.

l. The victim must be in apprehension of an *immediate* harmful or offensive contact. Therefore, the threat must be imminent. It must be impending or about to occur.

m. In *Case B*, Defendant intended to throw a rock in a stream; Defendant did not aim at or intend to scare Plaintiff in any way. Plaintiff ducked to miss being hit by the rock. Nonetheless, the court held that Defendant had general intent, which was sufficient to make out Plaintiff's assault claim.

n. We discussed two hypotheticals in which the threat was immediate. In the first one, the actor pointed a gun in the victim's direction. In the other one, the actor threw a punch at the victim and missed.

# — Chapter 5 —

# Analyzing Legal Problems

As early as Chapter 1, you were introduced to the steps to legal analysis and how to approach a legal problem using some basic facts and a fictitious dog biting law. In the subsequent chapters, you learned what role the reading and briefing of cases, note taking, and outlining play in legal analysis. This context was important to understanding how all aspects of law school learning relate to developing your legal reasoning skills. Now that you know what law school is all about, it is beneficial to revisit the specific steps to legal analysis in order to reinforce your understanding of it. This chapter will review the process using two examples: (1) a slightly modified version of Mr. Gerardi's problem from Chapter 1 and (2) a more complex problem involving a different issue, but related to the same legal topic—liability for injuries caused by a dog. Together these problems will allow you to further practice and sharpen your legal reasoning skills.

**Steps to Legal Analysis with Greater Detail**

1. *Isolate legal issues*
   a. *Identify undisputed issues*
   b. *Identify disputed issues*
2. *Research relevant law*
   a. *Read cases*
   b. *Synthesize legal rule*
3. *Apply rule to fact scenario*
4. *Resolve legal issues*

If you recall, Mr. Gerardi's case involved a question regarding his liability for injuries his dog, a Golden Retriever, caused to a child. For the analysis that follows, we will be looking to answer the same question, but we will pretend Mr. Gerardi's dog is a Rottweiler instead. We will keep the rest of the story the same. To review, the facts were as follows:

Mr. Gerardi was walking his unleased dog in a public park when the dog bit a young boy, causing injuries to the boy's leg. The boy was playing on the sidewalk, unaware of the dog, until the attack.

The boy sought medical attention from a local hospital's emergency room. His parents sent Mr. Gerardi the hospital bill along with a demand for reimbursement. According to your client, his dog is gentle; however, there was one prior incident in which the dog scratched a stranger. The stranger required no medical attention.

After a preliminary investigation into the matter, you find out that the incident took place in New York and learn these additional relevant facts:

Recently, the Center for Disease Control listed the Rottweiler as the second most likely breed of dog named in fatal human attacks. Also, Mr. Gerardi's dog has been known to growl and snap at passersby. Though there was only one prior incident involving a stranger, last year his dog bit his daughter while she was entering the house. Mr. Gerardi had to take his daughter to the hospital emergency room, where she received several stitches for a laceration to her leg.

To answer Mr. Gerardi's question, you will need to first examine the relevant law. Because the *Miletich*, *Illian*, and *Malpezzi* decisions from Chapter 2 are the most relevant, we will use them and their corresponding case annotations and case briefs to synthesize a rule. The general rule for when a dog owner is strictly liable for injuries caused by his or her dog is explicit in the cases and thus easy to write. Liability is triggered when: (a) the dog has vicious propensities and (b) the owner knew or should have known of such propensities. When you apply this general rule to the facts, it is clear that both elements are disputed, as they cannot be resolved without further analysis. This simple act completes the first step to analyzing this legal problem. We have identified the two disputed issues.

Instead of stating these issues generally, you should tailor them to include the specific, relevant facts of Mr. Gerardi's case. The first issue would then become whether Mr. Gerardi's dog, a Rottweiler that had previously scratched a stranger, bitten a family member, and growls and snaps at passersby, but is described by Mr.

Gerardi as gentle, has vicious propensities.  The second issue would be whether Mr. Gerardi knew or should have known of the dog's vicious propensities.

The next step is to synthesize rules from the cases that can resolve the issues. In other words, you want to figure out what factors a court weighs in deciding whether a dog has vicious propensities or the dog owner knew of such propensities. In Chapter 1, you were introduced to the concept of charting cases.  Charting cases is a good idea when you are dealing with multiple disputed issues and need an organized way to sort through those issues.  For Mr. Gerardi's problem, because all three cases address both issues, it is useful to create two charts, one for each issue.  You would pull the information for the charts from your case briefs. Specifically, you would devote a column to the following headings: case name, facts, court's decision, and reasoning.  These columns help you better see what bearing the individual facts had on the court's decision and why.  Below is what the chart of the *Miletich*, *Illian*, and *Malpezzi* cases would look like on the first issue.

| Case | Facts | Vicious Propensities? | Reasoning |
|------|-------|-----------------------|-----------|
| Miletich | Stranger approached dog owner's door while dog— Chow Chow breed—was tied & sleeping; stranger startled dog; dog then bit her twice on leg causing injuries; testimony = breed can be potentially aggressive; family pet since 8 weeks old; owned for 4 years w/o incident; dog was "nippy" and "territorial" when just several weeks old; owner routinely restrained dog to keep him from running away | No | Evidence that dog was "nippy" and "territorial" when just several weeks old not sufficient when owned as family pet for 4 years (since dog was 8 weeks old) w/o incident; the manner in which P-stranger was bitten does not support an inference that dog was aggressive b/c P never saw dog until immediately before she was bitten and dog was asleep and startled by P's presence. |
| Illian | Injured person was long-time acquaintance with dog | No | Evidence of barking, running, etc. when |

| | | | |
|---|---|---|---|
| | owners and knew dog well; interacted with dog often w/o problems; dog a mixed-breed; campground required that all dogs be leashed; dog owners testified that they owned dog since she was 5 weeks old; the dog had never bitten anyone, never acted aggressively, and they never received any complaints about the dog's behavior; neighbor testified that dog barked, jumped, and ran onto neighbor's property when she and husband drove in; campsite director testified that the dog frightened her by leaping off the porch, barking and running toward her as she walked past; dog growled at acquaintance's brother-in-law one month before incident; no complaints about the dog's behavior were ever lodged by neighbor, director or acquaintance's brother-in-law | | people drove or walked past was "typical territorial behavior"; the single instance of growling alleged also insufficient w/o other evidence. Here, dog owners had long history w/ dog w/o any incidences of aggression; injured acquaintance also had longstanding familiarity and contact with dog w/o any prior incidences of aggression |
| Malpezzi | Dog was an abandoned pit bull that D rescued; D owner believed that dog might have been dumped b/c he wasn't a "fighter"; for 2 months, dog interacted with D dog owner, his girlfriend and their children w/o incident; during that period, dog did not bark, growl or bare his teeth at, jump on or chase any person or animal or display any aggression toward anyone. Also, during that period, D dog owner did not receive any complaints from | No | The nature of the attack, which lacked provocation, alone is not sufficient to raise question as to dog's propensities; fact that dog was chained to property without more is not sufficient; neither is breed. When other facts suggesting aggressiveness are absent, these facts alone are not enough. |

| | anyone in the neighborhood about the dog; parties dispute whether dog was chained on D's property; while D owner was walking dog one day, he bit 6-yr-old P on his arm w/o provocation. | | |
|---|---|---|---|

Putting all of the relevant information from the three cases into this single document makes it easier to synthesize a rule. You no longer need to flip between case briefs to see what the court's pattern or recipe is for deciding the issue of vicious propensities. In this way, the rule almost jumps off the page. The rule is:

> Courts look at whether the dog has acted aggressively in the past. They consider whether the dog has previously jumped on or ran after passersby or cars, bitten, growled, snapped or bared its teeth at others. If such evidence exists, courts will also consider the ferocity of the breed of dog, nature of the attack, and fact that the dog was restrained in some fashion. However, absent such evidence, these facts on their own are insufficient to establish vicious propensities. Moreover, evidence that a dog is nippy, territorial, barks, or has even growled once before is insufficient on its own to establish vicious propensities.

The rule for knowledge of vicious propensities is equally obvious after charting the cases. The chart begins on the next page. The facts column is identical to the one in the first chart because the facts are either relevant or provide necessary context for both issues. That will not always be the case, however, particularly when the issues are distinct and do not overlap factually.

| Case | Relevant Facts | Knowledge of Vicious Propensities? | Reasoning |
|------|----------------|-----------------------------------|-----------|
| Miletich | Stranger approached dog owner's door while dog—Chow Chow breed—was tied & sleeping; stranger startled dog; dog then bit her twice on leg causing injuries; testimony = breed can be potentially aggressive; family pet since 8 weeks old; owned for 4 years w/o incident; dog was "nippy" and "territorial" when just several weeks old; owner routinely restrained dog to keep him from running away | No | Evidence that owner routinely restrained dog to keep him from running away does not support inference that owner was aware that dog might pose a danger. Breed alone, without other evidence, also not sufficient. |
| Illian | Injured person was long-time acquaintance with dog owners and knew dog well; interacted with dog often w/o problems; dog a mixed-breed; campground required that all dogs be leashed; dog owners testified that they owned dog since she was 5 weeks old; the dog had never bitten anyone, never acted aggressively, and they never received any complaints about the dog's behavior; neighbor testified that dog barked, jumped, and ran onto neighbor's property when she and husband drove in; campsite director testified that the dog frightened her by leaping off the porch, barking and running toward her as she walked past; dog growled at acquaintance's | No | No complaint ever made to owner about the dog's territorial behavior; never told about growling incident either; the fact that dog was tethered does not indicate knowledge b/c campground required it |

| | | | |
|---|---|---|---|
| | brother-in-law one month before incident; no complaints about the dog's behavior were ever lodged by neighbor, director or acquaintance's brother-in-law | | |
| Malpezzi | Dog was an abandoned pit bull that D rescued; D owner believed that dog might have been dumped b/c he wasn't a "fighter"; for 2 months, dog interacted with D dog owner, his girlfriend and their children w/o incident; during that period, dog did not bark, growl or bare his teeth at, jump on or chase any person or animal or display any aggression toward anyone. Also, during that period, D dog owner did not receive any complaints from anyone in the neighborhood about the dog; parties dispute whether dog was chained on D's property; while D owner was walking dog one day, he bit 6-yr-old P on his arm w/o provocation | No | Where there is no other evidence that owner knew of vicious propensities, dog's breed is irrelevant to analysis. |

Synthesizing what the court did in each of the cases leads to the following rule:

Courts will infer that an owner knows of his or her dog's vicious propensities when the dog has bitten someone before or where the owner received complaints that the dog has acted aggressively. Courts will also infer knowledge where the owner keeps the dog as a guard dog or restrains the dog out of concern that it might put others at risk of harm. However, simply restraining or leashing a dog to keep it from running away is not sufficient evidence of knowledge. Finally, courts will only consider ferocity of the dog's breed when other evidence of the owner's knowledge is present.

With these rules, the second step to legal analysis is complete. The third and final steps are to apply the rules to the facts and reach a conclusion on each issue. Because there are two issues, you would analyze one at a time. First, a court will likely decide that Mr. Gerardi's dog has vicious propensities. The dog has not only growled and snapped at strangers before, but also has injured two people. The dog scratched a stranger and bit Mr. Gerardi's own daughter, requiring her to receive stitches on her leg. Though Mr. Gerardi believes his dog to be gentle, Rottweilers— the breed of his dog—are extremely ferocious animals. Additionally, the dog attacked the young boy without provocation. Given that the dog has acted aggressively in the past, his breed and the nature of the attack are both relevant to the analysis.

Second, a court will likely also find that Mr. Gerardi had knowledge of his dog's vicious propensities. Though there is no evidence that Mr. Gerardi received complaints about his dog's behavior or restrained the dog, he knew of his dog's prior aggressive acts. He knew about the prior scratch involving the stranger as well as the bite of his own daughter. Given this knowledge, the fact that the Center for Disease Control listed the Rottweiler breed as the second most likely breed of dog named in human attacks is relevant. Accordingly, he was aware of his dog's vicious propensities.

The last step is to answer the client's question. Mr. Gerardi must pay the boy's medical expenses as the dog has vicious propensities and Mr. Gerardi was aware of them. As a result, he is liable for any injuries his dog caused to another.

This example should have brought it all together for you. It walked you from the reading, annotating, and briefing of cases to case charting and then to rule synthesis and application. These are the steps to legal analysis. They are what we used to solve a very typical law school exam problem.

Let's see how those same steps operate when analyzing a different factual scenario and new law on the same general topic. Assume you have a new client,

Ms. Levine, who is the owner of a multi-family home in Irvington, New York. She is an absentee owner because she herself does not reside there. Instead, she rents out both sides of the home to tenants. One of the tenants, Jack Goldsmith, has a family dog—a black German shepherd. Recently, the dog bit and injured a child who was visiting with the other tenant's children. The parents of the injured child have sued Ms. Levine under strict liability, seeking reimbursement for their child's medical bills as well as compensation for her pain and suffering. Ms. Levine has sought your advice on whether she is responsible in any way for the child's injuries.

Because your client is not a lawyer, she will likely be unable to define the legal issues and identify the relevant facts for you. In fact, as you saw with Mr. Gerardi, most clients will either inundate you with more facts than you need or give you insufficient facts. It is your job to sort through what the client tells you, setting aside any irrelevant information and eliciting more facts when necessary.

After more conversations with Ms. Levine, you learn the following additional information:

> Ms. Levine's lease with her tenant Jack Goldsmith specifically provides that the tenant is allowed to keep a dog on the property. As part of the lease agreement, the tenant is responsible for any property damage caused by the dog. In fact, Ms. Levine collected a pet security deposit in the amount of $250 for such damages. Because the property is shared by two tenants, they both have use of the lawn, which is about ¼ of an acre of property enclosed by a chain link fence.
>
> Ms. Levine knew that Mr. Goldsmith's dog was a black German shepherd. At the time of the lease, he explained that the dog had been part of his family for over 10 years and was nothing but a loving, obedient dog. Though Ms. Levine has not spent much time with the dog, she has had the occasion to see the dog, either playing outside or hanging out in the apartment, during her monthly visits to collect the rent as well as during the times she needed to attend to repairs on the property. Anytime the dog was outside, he

was chained to a stake in the ground. The dog sometimes barked at her when she visited. Several times the dog even growled and gnashed his teeth at her; however, she never felt threatened because, in each instance, the dog quickly responded to the tenant's command to "hush". Once or twice, she pet the dog without incident.

Ms. Levine has received complaints from neighbors and the other tenant about the dog defecating on her lawn as well as the neighboring lawns.

On the day of the incident, the dog was outside, but unchained. The other tenant, who was unaware that the dog was outside at the time, sent her three children and one of their playmates, Alison McElroy, who was six-years-old, outside to play. Moments later, she heard Alison scream. Alison was bit in the arm and needed to be rushed to the emergency room, where she received 19 stitches for her injuries. According to the children, the only eye-witnesses to the incident, the dog lunged at Alison as she was climbing the ladder to the swing set. The children did not see or hear the dog before that point.

After meeting with the client, assume that you researched the relevant law and found a handful of cases on point. The four most relevant ones are included at the end of this chapter. Though the client has posed the general question of whether she is strictly liable for the injuries caused by her tenant's dog, you still need to identify the legal issues that arise from this question—the first step to legal analysis. To do so, you will need a general understanding of the applicable law. The most helpful case in this regard is *Sarno*. Before moving on in this chapter, read and brief that case keeping your purpose in mind—that is, to understand the general law on the topic of a landlord's strict liability for injuries caused by his or her tenant's dog.

**Be sure to read and brief the *Sarno* case on page 100 before reading on**

From *Sarno*, you should have ascertained that a plaintiff must prove three elements to recover against a landlord on a theory of strict liability. Those elements, which were explicitly outlined in the case itself, are: (1) the landlord had notice that a dog was being harbored on the premises; (2) the landlord knew or should have known that the dog had vicious propensities; and (3) the landlord had sufficient control of the premises to allow the landlord to remove or confine the dog. Applying this general rule to Ms. Levine's circumstances, it is obvious that two of the elements are undisputed issues. Ms. Levine definitely had notice that the dog was on the premises—element 1—because she spoke to the tenant about the dog and allowed him to keep the dog on the property per a lease agreement that she executed.

Though the landlord had notice that the dog was on her property, she did not have sufficient control of the premises to allow her to remove or confine the dog. The facts here are virtually identical to the facts in *Sarno* on this element and thus warrant the same conclusion. Ms. Levine, like the landlord in *Sarno,* visited the property once a month to collect rent and at other times to check on the house in general. Therefore, assuming that Ms. Levine not only knew that the dog was on her property (element 1), but also that it had vicious propensities (element 2), she still would not be liable for the injuries because she did not have the requisite control over the property (element 3). The absence of that element is thus fatal to the plaintiff's claim of liability against Ms. Levine.

Even so, in practice and in law school, you would not end your analysis there. You still would analyze the remaining element—element 2—because you would want to build the best case for your client. Here, the more required elements there are that the plaintiff cannot satisfy the stronger case you would have. Also, if the court disagreed with your conclusion that the landlord did not have sufficient control over the premises, you would need to analyze the final element to continue to defend against the lawsuit. There is also a practical reason for completing the analysis: to demonstrate the full extent of your legal analysis skills. When your professor purposefully creates a disputed issue for you to resolve, you should resolve that issue even if it does not change your overall answer to the main question. Your professor is assessing your legal reasoning skills. If you do not reason through all of the disputed issues, he or she will not be able to do so. As a result, you will not receive full credit for your answer, even if it is the correct one.

Therefore, after having identified and resolved the undisputed issues, you are left to analyze the disputed issue—whether the landlord knew or should have known that the dog had vicious propensities. To tailor the issue to the client's situation, you would add specific facts to the issue statement. With those facts, the disputed issue would become:

> Whether Ms. Levine, who is an absentee landlord, knew or should have known that the dog had vicious propensities when she was told it was a German Shephard, had personally heard the dog's barking and on several occasions had even seen the dog growl and gnash its teeth, but never received any complaints about the dog injuring or attempting to harm anyone and was assured by the tenant that the dog was an obedient, kind, family dog.

Though there are more relevant facts to consider, this issue statement hones in on the most pertinent ones and identifies the facts weighing most heavily in favor and against the landlord's knowledge.

To resolve this disputed issue, you must first research the relevant law—the second step to legal analysis. Thus, you must re-read the *Sarno* case, the one that gave you the general rule for landlord liability, as well as read the other three cases at the end of this chapter (*Orozco, Smedley, Champ-Doran*) in order to synthesize a rule. Your new purpose is to figure out what a court looks at in deciding whether a landlord possesses knowledge of a dog's vicious propensities. Before moving on in this chapter, you should read all of the cases with this purpose in mind as well as brief the three new cases. Remember that you are only concerned about their holdings on the second element. Therefore, only those facts and reasoning relevant to resolving that element should be included in your case briefs.

**Be sure to read and brief the *Orozco, Smedley, Champ-Doran* cases beginning on page 102 and re-read *Sarno* before moving on**

Before settling on a specific rule, it is useful to examine each of the cases individually. First, in *Sarno*, the court held that the landlord did not have the requisite knowledge that the dog, a bull mastiff, had vicious propensities. The defendants—a husband and wife—were absentee landlords. The husband visited the property approximately once a month to collect rent and check on the house in general. On two occasions, he observed a bull mastiff on the property and, on at least one of those occasions he petted the dog on the head without incident. However, it is unknown whether the dog he observed was the same one that injured the infant plaintiff because the tenants owned two bull mastiffs at the time. The wife, on the other hand, never noticed any dogs during her visits to the property.

In *Orozco*, the landlord also did not have knowledge that the tenant's dog had vicious propensities despite the fact that other tenants in the building were frightened of the pit bull and that it had growled at the superintendent the day before the attack. The superintendent had never received complaints about the dog and never observed it acting aggressively. In fact, during his own encounters with the dog in the hallway, the dog passed him "at ease." The fact that the tenant allegedly tied the dog when it was in the apartment had no bearing since there was no evidence he did so out of fear that his dog would attack someone.

Similarly, in *Smedley*, the landlord did not have knowledge that the tenant's pit bull had any vicious propensities. The landlord was an absentee landlord in the truest sense; he visited the property at most once a year. And, even though his neighbors might have been aware that the dog was vicious, he did not know that the dog was even present on the property and he never received any complaints about the dog from the neighbors. Moreover, the presence of a "Beware of Dog" sign, by itself, was insufficient to impute the landlord with notice of the dog's vicious propensities.

However, in *Champ-Doran*, the landlord had the requisite knowledge. He knew of at least one of the tenant's two dogs and had received complaints from neighbors about the dogs' loud barking and lunging at people through holes in the fence on the property. He also knew that one of the dogs had previously escaped. By his own testimony he was definitely aware of the holes in the fence, but claimed he "didn't think any dog could get under" the fence. He had even previously warned the tenant that the "dogs had to go." Therefore, he had sufficient knowledge that the dogs at issue had vicious propensities.

If you were to chart the cases on this element, there would be a column for the case name, facts, holding, and reasoning. The chart, depicted below, provides a very good visual of the law from which you can distill a rule.

| Case | Facts | Knowledge? | Reasoning |
|---|---|---|---|
| Sarno | Ds-husband/wife-landlords; husband visited property once a month to collect rent and check on house; on 2 occasions he observed bull mastiff on property; on at least one of those occasions he petted dog w/o incident; he was unsure whether he observed same dog that injured boy b/c tenant had two bull mastiffs; the wife never noticed any dogs when she visited property | No | Landlords were absentee landlords; whatever limited experience they had with dog did not suggest that dog was aggressive |
| Orozco | D-landlord's superintendent testified that other tenants were frightened of pit bull; superintendent never received any complaints about dog and never observed the dog acting aggressively; when he encountered dog in hallway the dog passed him "at ease"; P testified that day before attack the dog had growled at him; tenant allegedly tied dog when it was in the apartment. | No | D landlord had no knowledge; he received no complaints; fact that dog was tied in apartment not relevant since there is no evidence that dog was restrained out of fear that dog would attack visitor |

| Smedley | D landlord visited property at most once a year; D did not know dog was present on property; D's neighbors knew that tenant's dog was vicious; tenant had placed "Beware of Dog" sign in her window. | No | D rarely visited property—a true absentee landlord; just because neighbors knew about dog, does not mean that landlord did; landlord never received any complaints about dog from neighbors or anyone else; the presence of the sign, standing alone, is insufficient |
|---|---|---|---|
| Champ-Doran | D landlord knew of at least one of tenant's two dogs; D received complaints from neighbors about dog's loud barking and lunging at people through holes in the fence on property; he knew that one dog had escaped before and warned tenant that the "dogs had to go"; D aware of holes in fence but "didn't think any dog could get under" fence | Yes | Had knowledge that dog was present and posed a danger to others; he was informed of the danger by complaints by neighbors; he also knew about the holes in his fence and the potential for the dogs escaping again |

After having closely examined all of the relevant precedent cases and charted them in this way, you are poised to synthesize a rule. You need to put together what happened in the cases to derive a rule that embraces them as well as the current problem. It seems that an absentee landlord who had little to no contact with the offending dog is not likely to be charged with knowledge even when other tenants or neighbors were concerned about the dog's viciousness so long as the landlord was not made aware of those concerns. A landlord's contact with the dog that is uneventful also weighs against having the required knowledge. It also seems that courts are not inclined to impute knowledge to a landlord when the only evidence of viciousness is that the dog growls on occasion, the dog is restrained for a reason other than out of fear of the dog's behavior or the owner posts "Beware of

Dog" signs on the property. Instead, the landlord needs to have personally witnessed the dog acting aggressively (i.e. loud barking, lunging at people) or received complaints to that effect or know there is a potential risk that the dog will escape from his or her property to be charged with knowledge of the dog's vicious propensities.

The preceding paragraph, with the exception of the first two sentences, is the synthesized rule. Notice that it is four sentences in length and, though it has some specific illustrations pulled from the precedent cases, it is generally applicable to other cases on the same issue. It effectively advises the reader as to the factors a court typically considers in deciding the issue of vicious propensities. A clear and comprehensive rule like this one is what is needed for your reader to understand the law and follow the reasoning for your conclusion.

Therefore, the next step to legal analysis—Step 3—is to apply this synthesized rule to the facts of the problem and conclude. In other words, you need to analyze your client's facts in light of the rule. As an absentee landlord, Ms. Levine has had little contact with the dog. (*Sarno*) Moreover, any contact she has had with the dog has been uneventful. (*Sarno*) Once or twice she petted the dog without incident. (*Sarno*) And, other than hearing him bark or observing him growl and gnash his teeth several times, Ms. Levine had never personally witnessed the dog acting aggressively. (*Orozco*) To the contrary, during the times where the dog growled or gnashed its teeth, the dog quickly responded to the tenant's command to "hush," which was entirely consistent with the tenant's report to the landlord at the time of the lease agreement that the dog was a loving, obedient dog and a fixture in the family for over 10 years.

Nor had Ms. Levine received any complaints about the dog's aggressiveness from the other tenant or anyone else. (*Orozco; Smedley; Champ-Doran*) The only complaints regarding the dog had to do with continual dog poop on the property and elsewhere. The fact that the dog was chained to a stake in the ground while outside, standing alone, is insufficient to impute knowledge to Ms. Levine. (*Orozco*) Therefore, it is unlikely that Ms. Levine had knowledge or should have had knowledge that the dog had vicious tendencies.

The preceding paragraphs not only apply the rule to the facts, but also implicitly reason by analogy to the cases. Reasoning by analogy to the rule cases shows the reader that you applied the rule appropriately. Your conclusion will be trusted because it is consistent with the holdings in cases with like facts and distinct from the cases with distinguishable facts. The case names in parenthesis in the earlier paragraphs identify the case or cases that you would have relied on in applying the rule. As you can tell, there are many similarities between Ms. Levine's problem and the facts in the analogous cases of *Sarno, Orozco,* and *Smedley* and a very important distinction from the facts in the distinguishing case of *Champ-Doran.* Unlike the absentee landlord in that case, Ms. Levine never received any complaints about the dog's aggressive behavior or tendency to escape. Therefore, Ms. Levine's problem is most in harmony with those cases in which the court held that the landlord lacked knowledge of the dog's viscous propensities.

The conclusion—that Ms. Levine similarly did not have the requisite knowledge—is the last step to legal analysis. The conclusion resolves the disputed issue for the reader. In this example, however, it does not answer the client's original question about whether she is responsible for the injuries her tenant's dog caused to the child. Because the parents of the child will be unable to prove two of the three necessary elements of their claim—knowledge of vicious propensities and control—she will most likely not be liable for the injuries. Your answer to the client's initial question is what completes your analysis of the problem. If this were a final exam question, you would have received the most points for your analysis of the disputed issue. But you would have secured an A if you addressed the undisputed ones and brought them all together in reaching the overall answer.

Through the two problems in this chapter, you now should see clearly the connection between all you do in law school and legal analysis. Whether it is your reading and briefing of cases or your synthesis and outlining of the course material, you are trying to understand the law so that you can solve legal problems. From the moment your client describes a problem, the process of legal analysis begins.

78 A.D. 3d 1157, 912 N.Y.S.2d 130

Supreme Court, Appellate Division, Second Department, New York.

Anthony SARNO, etc., et al., respondents,

v.

William B. KELLY, et al., appellants, et al., defendants.

Nov. 30, 2010

PETER B. SKELOS, J.P., RUTH C. BALKIN, RANDALL T. ENG, and LEONARD B. AUSTIN, JJ.

In a consolidated action to recover damages for personal injuries, etc., the defendants William B. Kelly and Regina Kelly appeal, as limited by their brief, from so much of an order of the Supreme Court, Suffolk County (Tanenbaum, J.) dated July 20, 2009, as denied that branch of their motion which was for summary judgment dismissing the cause of action sounding in strict liability insofar as asserted against them.

ORDERED that the order is reversed insofar as appealed from, on the law, with costs, and that branch of the appellants' motion which was for summary judgment dismissing the cause of action sounding in strict liability insofar as asserted against them is granted.

On the afternoon of March 8, 2002, a bull mastiff dog named Myron, owned by Barbara J. Claus, formerly known as Barbara Gassaway (hereinafter Claus), bit the infant plaintiff (hereinafter the infant) in his right thigh, while the infant was walking ahead of his mother immediately in front of their own driveway. Claus resided in a house directly across the street from the infant and his mother, which Claus rented from the appellants, William B. Kelly and Regina Kelly. Claus first acquired the dog approximately eight months prior to the attack and, on the day of the incident, also kept a second bull mastiff named Daisy at the rented house. It is undisputed that throughout the period of time that Myron was kept at the rented house, the appellants were absentee landlords.

To recover against a landlord for injuries caused by a tenant's dog on a theory of strict liability, the plaintiff must demonstrate that the landlord: (1) had notice that a dog was being harbored on the premises; (2) knew or should have known that the dog had vicious propensities, and (3) had sufficient control of the premises to allow the landlord to remove or confine the dog (*see Bard v. Jahnke,* 6 N.Y.3d 592, 815 N.Y.S.2d 16, 848 N.E.2d 463; *Ali v. Weigand,* 37 A.D.3d 628, 830 N.Y.S.2d 354).

The evidence submitted by the appellants in support of their motion, including, inter alia, their own deposition testimony, established their entitlement to judgment as matter of law (*see Ali v. Weigand,* 37 A.D.3d at 628, 830 N.Y.S.2d 354). William B. Kelly testified at his deposition that, during the period of time in question, he visited the rental house approximately once per month to collect rent and check on the house in general, and that, on two of those occasions, when he entered the house, he observed a bull mastiff present. He further testified that, on at least one of those occasions, he petted the dog on the head without incident. Thus, William B. Kelly established that he neither knew nor should have known that Myron had vicious propensities, and that he did not have sufficient control over the premises to allow him to remove or confine Myron. Regina Kelly testified that she visited the rental house approximately eight times in the two years prior to the incident, and that she knew what a bull mastiff looked like, but that she had never seen such a dog when she visited the house. Accordingly, she established that she did not have notice that a dog was being harbored at the rental house, and that she also did not have sufficient control over the premises.

In opposition to the appellants' showing, the plaintiffs failed to raise a triable issue of fact (*see* CPLR 3212(b)). Therefore, the Supreme Court should have granted the appellants' motion for summary judgment dismissing the strict liability cause of action insofar as asserted against them.

82 A.D.3d 48, 918 N.Y.S.2d 90

Supreme Court, Appellate Division, First Department, New York.

Juan OROZCO, Plaintiff–Appellant,

v.

725 S. BLVD., LLC, Defendant–Respondent.

March 8, 2011.

ANDRIAS, J.P., CATTERSON, MOSKOWITZ, ABDUS–SALAAM, ROMÁN, JJ.

Order, Supreme Court, Bronx County (Howard R. Silver, J.), entered October 21, 2009, which, to the extent appealed from as limited by the briefs, granted defendant's motion for summary judgment dismissing the complaint, unanimously affirmed, without costs.

Defendant landlord established prima facie that it neither knew nor had reason to know that the tenant's dog that attacked plaintiff had vicious propensities (*see Rivers v. New York City Hous. Auth.,* 264 A.D.2d 342, 694 N.Y.S.2d 57 (1999)). Although the building superintendent testified that the other tenants were frightened of the pit bull, he also said that he had never received any complaints about the animal or observed it acting aggressively and that during his own encounters with the dog in the hallway the dog passed him "at ease." In opposition, plaintiff failed to raise any issues of fact. His testimony that on the day before the attack the dog had growled at him does not support the inference that defendant knew or should have known of the dog's vicious propensities (*see Smith v. City of New York,* 68 A.D.3d 445, 889 N.Y.S.2d 187 (2009)). Nor is it significant that the tenant allegedly tied the dog when it was in the apartment, since there is no evidence that the tenant did so because he feared that the dog would attack a visitor (*see Collier v. Zambito,* 1 N.Y.3d 444, 447, 775 N.Y.S.2d 205, 807 N.E.2d 254 (2004)).

We have considered plaintiff's remaining arguments and find them unavailing.

21 A.D.3d 676, 799 N.Y.S.2d 682

Supreme Court, Appellate Division, Third Department, New York.

Victoria SMEDLEY, as Mother and Guardian of Jessica Smedley-McClay, an Infant, Appellant,

v.

Darrel ELLINWOOD, Respondent, et al., Defendant.

Aug. 11, 2005.

Before: CARDONA, P.J., CREW III, SPAIN, CARPINELLO and KANE, JJ.

CARDONA, P.J.

Appeal from an order of the Supreme Court (Kavanagh, J.), entered August 19, 2004 in Ulster County, which granted defendant Darrel Ellinwood's motion for summary judgment dismissing the complaint against him.

In December 2002, plaintiff's daughter suffered personal injuries when she was bitten by a pit bull owned by defendant Norleen Lamberty. Defendant Darrel Ellinwood is the owner and landlord of the premises where Lamberty resided at the time. Following the incident, plaintiff commenced this action alleging, inter alia, that Lamberty and Ellinwood had either actual or constructive notice of the dog's vicious propensities. Ellinwood successfully moved for summary judgment, prompting this appeal.

A landlord may be liable for the attack by a dog kept by a tenant if the landlord has actual or constructive knowledge of the animal's vicious propensities and maintains sufficient control over the premises to require the animal to be removed or confined (*see Strunk v. Zoltanski,* 62 N.Y.2d 572, 575, 479 N.Y.S.2d 175, 468 N.E.2d 13 (1984); *Mulhern v. Chai Mgt.,* 309 A.D.2d 995, 996, 765 N.Y.S.2d 694 (2003), *lv. denied* 1 N.Y.3d 508, 777 N.Y.S.2d 17, 808 N.E.2d 1276 (2004)). In support of his motion for summary judgment, Ellinwood submitted proof establishing, inter alia, that he rarely came to the residence, did not know that this particular dog was present at the premises and, additionally, had no knowledge of this dog's vicious propensities. Lamberty's deposition corroborated Ellinwood's statements. In response, plaintiff maintains that Ellinwood should have had notice of the dog's propensities inasmuch as Lamberty's neighbors had such knowledge. Furthermore, plaintiff asserts that the fact that Lamberty placed a "Beware of Dog" sign in her window should have been sufficient to constitute constructive notice to Ellinwood.

The fact that others may have been on notice of the dog's allegedly vicious nature does not establish that Ellinwood, who, at most, visited the premises once a year and received no complaints from the neighbors, was similarly on notice (*cf. Woodman v. Rosier,* 1 A.D.3d 1033, 1034, 767 N.Y.S.2d 182 (2003); *Brundrige v. Howes,* 259 A.D.2d 895, 896, 686 N.Y.S.2d 530 (1999); *Dixon v. Frazini,* 188 A.D.2d 1054, 592 N.Y.S.2d 208 (1992)). Additionally, the presence of a "Beware of Dog" sign, standing alone, is insufficient to impute notice of a dog's viciousness (*see Shaw v. Burgess,* 303 A.D.2d 857, 858-859, 756 N.Y.S.2d 362 (2003); *Shannon v. Schultz,* 259 A.D.2d 937, 938, 686 N.Y.S.2d 906 (1999), *lv. denied* 93 N.Y.2d 816, 697 N.Y.S.2d 563, 719 N.E.2d 924 (1999)). Given the absence in this record of actual or constructive notice, any issue as to the scope of Ellinwood's control over the premises is academic. Accordingly, Supreme Court properly granted Ellinwood's motion for summary judgment dismissing the complaint against him.

ORDERED that the order is affirmed, with costs.

CREW III, SPAIN, CARPINELLO and KANE, JJ., concur.

69 A.D.3d 1101, 892 N.Y.S.2d 665

Supreme Court, Appellate Division, Third Department, New York.

Andrew CHAMP-DORAN, Individually and as Parent and Guardian of Quentin Champ-Doran, an Infant, Respondent,

v.

Daniel LEWIS, Appellant.

Jan. 14, 2010.

Before: CARDONA, P.J., LAHTINEN, KAVANAGH, McCARTHY and GARRY, JJ.

CARDONA, P.J.

Appeal from a judgment of the Supreme Court (Work, J.), entered September 25, 2008 in Ulster County, which denied defendant's motion for summary judgment dismissing the complaint.

Plaintiff commenced this action seeking damages for injuries sustained by his son when he was attacked on the front porch of his home by one of the two dogs owned by defendant's tenant. Apparently, the dogs escaped from the fenced backyard of defendant's property. According to plaintiff's bill of particulars, defendant was not only aware of the vicious tendencies of his tenant's dogs, but also had actual and constructive notice that the fence surrounding his property was "broken and otherwise defective." Defendant denied these allegations and, following joinder of issue, moved for summary judgment dismissing the complaint. Supreme Court denied the motion, prompting this appeal.

Defendant maintains that since it is undisputed that the incident did not occur on his property, Supreme Court erred in denying his summary judgment motion. Generally, landlords do "not owe a duty of care" (*Terrio v. Daggett,* 208 A.D.2d 1163, 1163, 617 N.Y.S.2d 585 (1994)) to persons injured by a tenant's dog where the injury occurs off the landlord's premises (*see e.g. Seiger v. Dercole,* 50 A.D.3d 1524, 856 N.Y.S.2d 771, 856 N.Y.S.2d 771 (2008); *Ruffin v. Dykes,* 37 A.D.3d 1191, 830 N.Y.S.2d 426 (2007); *Braithwaite v. Presidential Prop. Servs., Inc.,* 24 A.D.3d 487, 806 N.Y.S.2d 681 (2005); *Shen v. Kornienko,* 253 A.D.2d 396, 676 N.Y.S.2d 593 (1998)). However, liability can nevertheless be imposed where it is established "that the defendant knew of the dog's presence on the premises and its vicious propensities, and that the defendant had control of the premises or otherwise had the ability to remove or confine the dog" (*Phillips v. Coffee To Go,* 269 A.D.2d 123, 124, 703 N.Y.S.2d 13 (2000) (internal quotation marks and citation omitted); *see Cronin v. Chrosniak,* 145 A.D.2d 905, 906, 536 N.Y.S.2d 287 (1988); *see also Dufour v. Brown,* 66 A.D.3d 1217, 888 N.Y.S.2d 219 (2009)).

Here, viewing the record evidence in the light most favorable to plaintiff, there is sufficient proof for purposes of this motion that defendant had knowledge of the dogs' vicious propensities, as well as an adequate opportunity to control the premises and properly confine the dogs (*see Meyers v. Haskins,* 140 A.D.2d 923, 924-925, 528 N.Y.S.2d 738 (1988)). Even crediting defendant's deposition testimony that he did not know about the dogs at the time he initially rented the property, he acknowledged being aware of at least one of them soon thereafter and admitted that a neighbor complained to him regarding loud barking. He also testified that he knew of a previous time that one of the dogs escaped and told the tenant that the "dogs had to go." Notably, the record contains affidavits from several neighbors indicating that, prior to the subject incident, they had notified defendant of the dogs' vicious behavior, such as continually barking and lunging at people through holes in defendant's fence. Defendant stated that he was aware of the holes in the fence but "didn't think any dog could get under." In our view, this and other proof sufficiently raised factual issues as to whether defendant breached a duty of care owed to persons who would be foreseeably injured by the escaping dogs. Therefore, defendant's motion for summary judgment dismissing the complaint was properly denied.

ORDERED that the judgment is affirmed, with costs.

LAHTINEN, KAVANAGH, McCARTHY and GARRY, JJ., concur.

# Chapter 5 Exercise:

Since your handling of Ms. Levine's case, you have developed an expertise in the area of dog owner liability for injuries caused by pets. Your new client, Sandra McDonald, heard about you through word-of-mouth and has sought your advice on whether she is responsible for injuries caused by her tenant's Rottweiler. The dog lunged at Anthony Vitello, the mailman, while he was delivering the tenant's mail. The dog then bit him several times, causing severe lacerations to his right arm and face. Mr. Vitello has demanded that Ms. McDonald compensate him for his medical expenses and pain and suffering.

Ms. McDonald is the owner of a multi-family house in Yonkers, New York. She is an absentee owner, but she visits the property at least once a month to collect rent and take care of any maintenance issues. She knew that her tenant, Jeremy Fox, had a dog; though she was not certain what type of dog it was, she suspected that it was a Rottweiler based on its look and size. With the exception of two or three times when the dog growled at her when she approached the house, the dog was very quiet and even-tempered. Her other tenant complained about the dog once when Mr. Fox first moved in, stating that she was not a "dog lover" and in fact was very afraid of dogs. To appease the tenant, Ms. McDonald asked Mr. Fox to keep his dog leashed at all times when outside. He agreed and, as far as she knew, complied. Ms. McDonald never received any other complaints about the dog from the tenant or anyone else.

Through the course of this dispute, Ms. McDonald has learned that the dog had previously bitten someone while off the property just six months earlier. That incident was reported in a headline story in the Yonkers Observer, the town's local paper. The story named Mr. Fox as the dog's owner. Even though Ms. McDonald receives and usually reads the Observer, she never saw the story.

Using the four cases in this chapter and a new case that follows, *Georgianna,* analyze whether Ms. McDonald will be strictly liable for Mr. Vitello's injuries. As you work on the problem, follow the steps to legal analysis and answer the following questions.

1. State the undisputed elements and explain why they are undisputed.

2. Identify the disputed element.

3. Synthesize a rule for the disputed element using the five cases. To get there, you should brief and chart all of the cases on this element.

4. Apply the rule to the facts and explain your reasoning.

5. Predict an outcome on the disputed element.

6. Answer the client's question.

126 Misc. 2d 766, 483 N.Y.S.2d 892

New York Supreme Court, Onondaga County

Mary A. Georgianna, Individually and on Behalf of Her Son, Richard Neuser, an Infant, Plaintiff,

v.

Sady Gizzy et al., Defendants

November 23, 1984

John R. Tenney, J.

Plaintiff's minor son was bitten by a dog owned by defendant Gizzy, on premises leased to Gizzy by defendants Quinn. The Quinns move for summary judgment contending that as absentee landlords, they are not liable for the actions of their tenant's dog.

Generally, a landlord not in possession of the premises is not liable for injuries inflicted by a tenant's dog. However, he may become liable if he has (1) actual knowledge of the animal's vicious propensities and (2) has retained substantial control over the premises. (*Zwinge v. Love*, 37 AD2d 874.)

Since there is a dispute over the issue of control of the premises, it may not be decided by summary judgment. The issue which must be addressed by the court is that of actual knowledge "of the vicious propensities". There is no dispute from the affidavits -- the Quinns had no actual knowledge. Plaintiff argues that they had "constructive notice", and it is the same thing and meets the *Zwinge v. Love* (*supra*) requirements.

Plaintiff offers evidence that the dog had previously bitten someone, and that a report of the incident was filed with the Town of Salina and the Onondaga County Department of Health. Plaintiff contends that this filed report constitutes constructive notice of the animal's vicious propensities. He cites *Strunk v. Zoltanski* (96 AD2d 1074, *aff'd* 62 NY2d 572), as authority. It is not. In that case, the landlord retained no control over the demised premises. However, he had actual knowledge of the dog's vicious nature not only prior to the incident, but prior to letting the premises.

The court held that the prior knowledge imposed a burden upon the landlord to refuse to lease or accept the consequences. Thus, a landlord who leases to a tenant knowing the tenant is an owner of a potentially dangerous dog will be responsible for any damage caused to a third party by the dog.

On the other hand, the issue of constructive notice and its effect on the actual notice requirement in the *Zwinge v. Love* case (*supra*) should be resolved. "'Constructive notice ordinarily means that a person should be held to have knowledge of a certain fact because he knows other facts from which it is concluded that he actually knew, or ought to have known, the fact in question. Constructive notice also exists whenever it is shown that reasonable diligence would have produced actual notice.' (42 N.Y. Jur., Notice and Notices, § 3.)" (*Bierzynski v. New York Cent. R. R. Co.*, 31 AD2d 294, 297.) Here, the fact in question is the vicious nature of the dog and the "other facts" are the defendants' knowledge of the existence of a dog and the filed dog bite report. Under these circumstances, was there a duty on the part of the landlord to exercise "reasonable diligence" which would necessarily include a search of public records? "The question is not only whether an inquiry would have revealed the fact, but also whether, acting as an ordinarily prudent person would have done, the person to be charged was called upon, under the circumstances, to make inquiry." (42 NY Jur, Notice and Notices, § 17; *see, Anderson v. Blood*, 152 NY 285.)

Although the Quinns knew of the existence of a dog, it did not create a duty to inquire further. Such a burden would be oppressive and unreasonable. "[N]ot all relationships give rise to a duty. One should not be held legally responsible for the conduct of others merely because they are within our sight or environs ... While a court might impose a legal duty where none existed before ... such an imposition must be exercised with extreme care". (*Pulka v. Edelman*, 40 NY2d 781, 785-786.)

Similarly, the mere existence of the filed report created no duty. Absent some statutory provision, records kept by or for governmental entities are not notice to the public. (*Dunn v. City of New York*, 205 NY 342; *Curnen v. Mayor, Aldermen & Commonalty of City of N. Y.*, 79 NY 511.) Here, no statutory provision is claimed. Thus, there is no duty to inquire and no constructive notice. The motion for summary judgment should, therefore, be granted.

# The Art of Communication:
# Writing Your Analysis of a Legal Issue

Though the ability to analyze legal problems is important, it will go unnoticed in law school and in practice if you are unable to communicate your analysis in writing. The most prevalent form of writing in law school is writing for an exam. Not surprisingly, writing an exam answer is analogous to the type of writing covered in most first-year legal writing courses. Doctrinal and skills courses share the common goal of training you to think and ultimately write like a lawyer. Thus, you should pay close attention in your writing classes and take advantage of every opportunity to improve your writing there, as it will directly impact your exam writing skills.

The type of writing required on exams will either be *predictive* or *persuasive* writing. Predictive writing is writing that asks you to predict the likely outcome of a legal problem. This is usually the type of writing covered in first semester first-year writing courses where the end project is to write an interoffice legal memorandum. In contrast, persuasive writing is writing that asks you to argue that a certain outcome is the right one. This is usually the type of writing covered in second semester first-year writing courses where the main assignment is to write an appellate brief or trial brief or both. Whether the exam question demands a predictive or persuasive answer, the way you organize your analysis will be essentially the same. And, in both instances, you must be able to communicate your analysis in a helpful way. This requires that your answer be complete, concise, and clear.

Though your professors know the relevant law and pertinent facts of the questions they ask on exams, they will pretend not to when grading your exam answers. Instead, they will simulate a typical legal reader—a busy lawyer, who is knowledgeable in the law generally, but unfamiliar with the law that pertains to your particular legal question and uncertain about how that question will likely be resolved by a court. Thus, a conclusion alone, even if correct, will not impress your professors. They expect your answers to clearly and summarily explain the basis for your conclusion as well as the details on how you arrived there. To ensure that your answers do this, you must be methodical in your approach by first presenting the law and then discussing its application to the facts at issue.

## The IRAC Paradigm

To help teach you how to organize your analysis of a legal problem in writing, law professors have developed paradigms for law students to follow. The most popular one is IRAC, which stands for Issue, Rule, Application, and Conclusion. Law professors use paradigms other than IRAC, including, for example, CRAC (Conclusion, Rule, Application, Conclusion), CREAC (Conclusion, Rule, Explanation, Application, Conclusion) and BARAC (Bold Assertion, Rule, Application, Conclusion). The particular acronym used does not matter; they are all the same at their core. They share the common feature of first identifying the issue and then explaining the relevant legal principle before applying it to reach a conclusion. Also, they all require that you prove that the legal principle is legitimate and your application of the law is both correct and appropriate. The only real difference between the various paradigms is the labels used to show you how to accomplish these goals.

Because IRAC is the most universal paradigm as well as the core structure of most others, it is a good starting point for any draft. For exams, you should always ask your professors if they would like you to follow a different paradigm. In the absence of such an instruction, you should stick with IRAC and manipulate it as necessary.

The IRAC paradigm—law followed by application—is counter to the order in which beginner law students typically "discover" the answer and thus can be challenging to grasp at first. A student's discovery usually follows these steps: reading each case, examining all of the information (relevant and irrelevant) contained within them, synthesizing the cases, distilling a rule, and then applying the rule to the facts at issue in order to reach a conclusion. In contrast, in the written analysis, the legal reader expects to see a statement of the issue or conclusion first, followed by the rule and an explanation of it (including only the relevant information from the cases), and then an application to the question posed. Therefore, when it comes time to write the analysis, you must avoid organizing the material in the order in which you learned it. Instead, you should adhere to the IRAC formula or a similar paradigm, as they are designed specifically to meet your reader's expectations.

## The Issue

The "I" in IRAC stands for Issue. A good analysis first states the narrow legal question raised by the facts. If it is helpful for you to use the word "issue" in your statement, do so. For example, the issue statement for Mr. Gerardi's problem in Chapter 5 can be written as follows:

> At issue is whether Mr. Gerardi's Rottweiler, which he describes as gentle, but has previously scratched a stranger, bitten a family member, and growls and snaps at passersby, has vicious propensities under New York law.

Notice how the same sentence can be stated as a conclusion:

> Mr. Gerardi's Rottweiler, which he describes as gentle, but has previously scratched a stranger, bitten a family member, and growls and snaps at passersby, has vicious propensities under New York law.

This example effectively communicates the issue and most relevant facts while also previewing the conclusion.

It is perfectly acceptable to conclude at the beginning. Legal readers are typically busy and looking to be educated on the facts and applicable law quickly so that they can take action based on your prediction. Thus, they want you to be upfront about your conclusion and expect that your analysis will be organized around that conclusion. They do not expect a "ta-da" moment in your writing. In fact, writing that is purposefully suspenseful will only annoy legal readers and ultimately make them question the validity of your conclusion.

# The Rule

The "R" in IRAC stands for Rule. Here is where you state the rule of law that applies to the legal question raised by the facts. It is the legal proposition that you synthesized from the case law or that comes out of a statute that controls how the issue should be resolved. It is important to remember that you need not state the rule in a single sentence or in some formulaic way. In fact, the rule might list elements or conditions that must exist for establishing a claim, crime, or defense. It might also list factors that courts typically consider or balance in resolving the issue. In other words, identify the pattern or "recipe" that the courts follow in resolving issues like yours and explain it clearly. The length and depth of that explanation will vary depending on the issue and particular facts of your case.

If you were to present a rule for the issue statement to Mr. Gerardi's problem from earlier, you would write it as follows:

> In deciding a dog's vicious propensities, New York courts will look at whether the dog has exhibited aggressive behavior in the past. For example, they will consider whether the dog has previously jumped on or run after passersby or cars, bitten, growled, snapped or bared its teeth at others. If such evidence exists, courts will also consider the ferocity of the breed of dog, the manner in which the person was injured, and the fact that the dog was restrained. However, absent such evidence, these factors on their own are insufficient to establish vicious propensities. Moreover, evidence that a dog is nippy, territorial, barks, or has even growled once before is insufficient on its own to establish vicious propensities.

This is the rule synthesized from the *Miletich, Illian,* and *Malpezzi* cases in Chapter 2. As discussed before, your explanation of the rule should move from a statement of the general legal principle to the more narrow or specific ones, as is done here.

After stating the rule, you will need to support it by citing to and discussing the legal authority that validates it. In most instances, that authority will include a statute or rule cases—the cases you used to synthesize the rule—or a combination of both (when the language of a statute must be interpreted by the courts). The purpose of this section is to show that the rule has legal support. Some rules are easy to support because they are stated explicitly in a case or statute. If that is the situation, all you will need to do is cite the supporting source after the rule. You may also quote the relevant parts of that source if the quoted language is illuminating.

When your rule is a synthesized one, however, you must show that you correctly derived it from the cases. You must prove that your rule is right by explaining what happened in the rule cases. The general rule is that you should begin by discussing the cases that are most like the problem you have to solve. These are called analogous cases—cases with holdings like the one you are predicting. You should explain the distinguishing cases—cases with holdings that differ from the one you are predicting—second. The exception to this approach is when a distinguishing case provides the best support for the rule. There is a mix of possibilities that might make this so; it might happen when, for example, the distinguishing case is a leading case or mandatory authority, explains in depth the reasoning or policy for the rule, or has facts that shed light on how to appropriately apply the rule. Whether you discuss an analogous or distinguishing case first, you should always keep the like cases—cases with similar holdings—together to avoid jumping between diverse rulings.

To convince the legal reader as to the legitimacy of the rule, the rule explanation must include a discussion of the relevant facts, holding, and reasoning of each rule case. For the rule on vicious propensities, this would mean that you would explain all three rule cases: the *Miletich, Illian*, and *Malpezzi* decisions. An illustration of how your rule explanation of one of these cases, *Malpezzi*, might read is as follows:

> In *Malpezzi*, the court held that there was insufficient evidence
> that a pit bull that bit a six-year-old boy without provocation while his
> owner was walking him had vicious propensities. Despite the fact
> that the pit bull breed is known to be aggressive, there was no

evidence that this particular dog was aggressive. For the two-month period before the attack during which the owner cared for the dog, the dog did not exhibit any aggressive behavior. To the contrary, he interacted with the owner, his girlfriend, and their children without incident. Moreover, during that time, he did not bark, growl or bare his teeth at, jump on or chase any person or animal. Nor did the owner receive any complaints about the dog. Even if the dog was chained on the property, a fact the parties disputed, without any other evidence of vicious propensities, that fact, the nature of the attack, and breed alone were insufficient to raise a triable issue of fact on this element.

Through this explanation, your reader should be able to see how at least part of the rule developed. Once you explained all three cases, one after the other, the reader would also see how the rule works under different fact scenarios. A well-written explanation will establish that the rule is an accurate summary of the law that resolves the issue; it is neither too narrow, nor too broad, nor misleading in any way.

For an exam answer, your professor might not require that you cite authority or explain the rule cases in this fashion. Your professor might be interested in a statement of the relevant rule only. The extent to which you will need to explain or support the rule will depend on the professor as well as the type of exam. Nonetheless, as covered in Chapter 4 on outlining, you will need to know the rule cases, even if you do not write about them, as they are instructive on how to apply the rule appropriately. Thus, you will be using them, even if just implicitly, in your application of the rule. In formal legal writing, however, such as an internal legal office memorandum, you will most certainly be expected to provide a citation to and explanation of the relevant authority so that your reader could check the accuracy of your rule statement.

## The Application

The "A" in IRAC stands for Application. It is a statement of whether the facts of the case satisfy the rule. Thus, the statement necessarily includes the language of the rule. Here is how the application section would be written for Mr. Gerardi's problem:

> Mr. Gerardi's dog has vicious propensities because it exhibited aggressive behavior in the past. The dog has not only growled and snapped at strangers before, but also has injured two people. Because there is other evidence of the dog's aggressiveness, the dog's dangerous breed—a Rottweiler—is not only relevant, but further supports the conclusion that his dog has vicious propensities.

In short, it is essentially your conclusion plus a brief explanation supporting that conclusion.

Just like you must prove that the rule is accurate by supporting it with authority, you must also prove that your application of the rule is correct by explaining how that authority supports your conclusion. When there are rule cases, this means that you must demonstrate that your conclusion is consistent with the holdings in those cases. You will compare the facts of your problem to the facts in the rule cases. For the analogous cases, you will show how the similarities in circumstances justify the same result for your problem. For the distinguishing cases, you will show the opposite—how the differences in circumstances merit a different conclusion. You will examine only the similarities and differences in facts that matter—facts that determined the outcome of the cases—and ignore the inconsequential or irrelevant ones.

Moreover, your case comparisons must not simply list the similarities or differences between your problem and the rule cases; rather, the comparisons must illustrate how they support one conclusion over the other. Therefore, it is not the number of similar or dissimilar facts between your problem and a rule case that determine the outcome, but instead how significant or important they are in the court's analysis of the issue. Thus, you must not compare facts in a vacuum; you must simultaneously apply any policy and reasoning from the rule cases too. The general rule for this section is to reason by analogy to analogous cases before distinguishing ones, mirroring the order in the rule explanation section, unless an exception, as discussed earlier, warrants otherwise. The case comparison to the *Malpezzi* case—the case explained earlier in support of the rule—would be as follows:

> In stark contrast to the pit bull in *Malpezzi*, Mr. Gerardi's Rottweiler did not interact with his family and others without incident. The dog has a history of aggressive behavior. The dog not only scratched a stranger before, but it also previously bit Mr. Gerardi's own daughter, requiring her to receive stitches on her leg. Though Mr. Gerardi believes his dog to be gentle, he is not. Rottweilers can be extremely ferocious animals and Mr. Gerardi's dog seems to be no exception. Given that the dog has acted aggressively in the past, his breed, unlike the pit bull's in *Malpezzi*, is relevant to the analysis. His breed together with the other evidence establishes that Mr. Gerardi's dog has vicious propensities.

The reasoning by analogy section is also the most appropriate place to present any opposing facts or counterarguments that are reasonably supported by the authority. In the above example, the fact that Mr. Gerardi described his dog as gentle was a fact weighing against the conclusion. It is included in the analysis, but quickly dismissed because it is outweighed by the other factors. Beginning sentences with the words "Though" or "Even though" is a good way to introduce and then rebut an opposing fact.

The same technique can be used for addressing counterarguments. To understand why a counterargument is unpersuasive, however, you must also explain the point of the argument. Then, you must quickly demonstrate how that argument is outweighed by the facts and reasoning supporting the conclusion. Keep in mind that you would develop a counterargument in this way only if it had a legitimate basis. If there is no or little basis for the argument, you should not waste the reader's time by writing that the opposition will argue a contrary point. Such statements are obvious and void of any analysis.

Similar to the rule explanation section, you might not need to include a complete reasoning by analogy segment for the exam, particularly if your professor does not expect you to discuss the relevant cases in defense of the rule. Even if not required, you will reason by analogy implicitly in supporting your application. Moreover, you will most certainly present a written analogical reasoning segment in formal legal writing assignments, like the internal legal office memorandum. Therefore, it is worthwhile understanding its function.

## The Conclusion

As discussed earlier, your conclusion, the "C" in IRAC, even if not stated explicitly at the start of the paradigm, should not be a surprise to the reader. After you have stated the rule and applied it to your problem, the conclusion should be obvious. For Mr. Gerardi's problem, it is clear: his dog has vicious propensities. If you were writing this conclusion, you might use an introductory word or phrase, such as "therefore," "thus," "hence," "accordingly," "in conclusion," or "in summary," to signal it. By re-stating the conclusion at the end of the paradigm, you complete your analysis.

## Pulling it All Together and Multi-Issue Problems

Not surprisingly, in practice, it is rare that a single set of facts raises only one legal question. More often a client's problem, as illustrated by Mr. Gerardi's and other sample problems throughout this book, raises multiple issues, even if some of them are undisputed. In the end, all of the issues, disputed and undisputed ones, must be evaluated in order to fully address a client's problem. You will accomplish this by writing an IRAC for every *disputed* issue and then writing a thesis or umbrella paragraph that connects the undisputed and disputed issues. The thesis or umbrella paragraph is where you will bring it all together and present your overall conclusion.

Before discussing how to write that paragraph, it is helpful to look back at Mr. Gerardi's problem, but this time using the simplified facts and fictitious law from Chapter 1. To recap, in that earlier version, Mr. Gerardi wanted to know whether he was responsible to pay the medical expenses of a child who was injured by his dog, a Golden Retriever, which was unleashed and in a public park. Other than scratching someone before, there were no other incidences of injury. Further, according to the law from that chapter, a dog owner would be liable for such injuries if: (1) the dog was dangerous; (2) the dog was not on the owner's real property; and (3) the dog is either unleashed or unmuzzled or both. It turned out that elements 2 and 3 were undisputed in Mr. Gerardi's case because there was no question that the dog was on public property and was both unleashed and unmuzzled at the time of the incident. Because these conclusions are obvious in light of the facts, there is no analysis to explain. Consequently, there is no need to write an IRAC on them. Instead, conclusions on undisputed issues like these can be presented in a few short sentences in the thesis or umbrella paragraph.

To drive home the point that an IRAC is unnecessary for undisputed issues, look at how an IRAC on undisputed element #2 would read:

**Issue:**

The issue is whether the dog was on the owner's real property.

**Rule:**

The dog must be on the owner's real property to avoid liability.

**Application:**

The dog was not on the owner's real property because it was on the public street.

**Conclusion:**

Therefore, the dog was not on the owner's real property.

You can quickly see that there is much redundancy in this IRAC. The Issue, Rule, and Conclusion are all straightforward and easily understood by reading the Application sentence alone. That sentence more than adequately tells the reader that the element was satisfied and why. As such, there is no need to bore the reader with an expanded IRAC—one that merely repeats the same information over and over again. Therefore, the Application part of the IRAC paradigm is usually sufficient to explain your conclusion on undisputed issues.

Only disputed issues, like whether the dog was dangerous (element 1), entail a deep analysis and thus require further textual explanation. To ensure that your explanation on disputed issues is organized and clear, you should follow the IRAC paradigm. If there are multiple disputed issues, you should keep them separate and write an IRAC for each one. The thesis or umbrella paragraph is where you will tie together multiple disputed issues as well as address the undisputed ones. An example of how the IRAC for element 1 would read is as follows:[11]

**Issue:**

The issue is whether Mr. Gerardi's dog is dangerous.

**Rule:**

In deciding whether a dog is dangerous, courts will look at whether the dog has previously injured another person in an unprovoked attack and the extent of those injuries. In the absence of a prior incident resulting in serious injuries caused directly from an attack, a dog that injures another person when unprovoked will not be considered a "dangerous" dog within the meaning of the statute. Moreover, the mere existence of a prior incident in which normal playful dog behavior results in a minor injury to another is not enough to establish dangerousness.

**Rule Explanation:**

In the *Dog Scratcher* case, the dog at issue had a history of getting excitable around strangers, but had never injured anyone before. Thus, the court found that the dog was not dangerous within the meaning of the statute. Similarly, the dog in the *Dog Biter* case was not dangerous. Even though there was a prior incident in which the dog barked and jumped on another person's legs, causing that person to fall and scrape her knees, the injury was very minor and an indirect result of typical dog behavior, not any unprovoked aggression.

In contrast, in the *Dog Attacker* case, the dog attacked another person six months prior to the incident at issue directly causing extensive and serious injury to the person's face and arms. Thus, the court found that the dog was dangerous. Similarly, in the *Killer Dog* case, the dog at issue maimed another person two years prior to the incident in question. Further, the testimony revealed that the dog had a

---

[11] This IRAC includes a full rule explanation and reasoning by analogy using the fictitious cases described in Chapter 1.

"killer instinct." As such, the dog was a dangerous dog, causing the type of injury the statute was intended to protect against.

### Application & Reasoning by Analogy:

The prior incident in which Mr. Gerardi's dog injured a stranger does not fit the conditions for dangerousness. The prior incident did not involve an unprovoked attack, but rather a scratch, which is typical of dogs, even gentle ones. Moreover, the incident resulted in a minor injury—a scratch—and not a serious injury, like in the *Killer Dog* and the *Dog Attacker* cases. In other words, Mr. Gerardi's situation is most similar to the facts in the *Dog Biter* case and very distinguishable from the *Dog Attacker* and the *Killer Dog* cases.

### Conclusion:

Thus, Mr. Gerardi's dog is likely not a "dangerous" dog within the meaning of the statute.

\*\*\*

If Mr. Gerardi's problem was an exam question, the professor would be most interested in your conclusion on the disputed issue of dangerousness and how you resolved it because that is where the bulk of the analysis was. Because disputed issues are the ones that involve in-depth legal reasoning, professors will typically award the most points for your work on them. Nonetheless, a question that raises undisputed issues would be incomplete if you did not address them as well. Returning to Mr. Gerardi's case, he asked whether he would have to pay the medical bills of the injured child, not whether his dog would be considered dangerous within the meaning of the statute. To give a complete response, you will need to bring together your answer on this disputed issue with your answers on the undisputed ones. The thesis or umbrella paragraph is where you would do just that.

This paragraph will explain to your reader what the general applicable law is and how you arrived at the disputed and undisputed issues. You should follow these general steps. First, you should state the general applicable law. Second, you should identify and conclude on the undisputed issues, providing a brief explanation of your basis for each conclusion. Even though the explanations should be short, they should also be complete, as you will not discuss the undisputed issues anywhere else in your answer. Third, you should identify and conclude on the disputed issues, also providing a succinct explanation of your support. Remember to keep these explanations brief because you will be discussing the disputed issues in-depth in the IRAC analysis that will follow. Finally, you should state your overall conclusion or answer to the problem. Here is how the thesis or umbrella paragraph would read for Mr. Gerardi's question of liability:

## Step 1 – State General Applicable Law

According to the relevant dog biting statute, a dog owner is liable for the injuries his dog caused to another if: (1) the dog was dangerous; (2) the dog was not on the owner's real property; and (3) the dog is either unleashed or unmuzzled or both.

## Step 2 - Identify and Conclude on Undisputed Issues

Mr. Gerardi's dog was not on his property, as he was on public property. Moreover, his dog was neither leashed nor muzzled.

## Step 3 – Identify and Conclude on Disputed Issues

Thus, the only disputed issue is whether his dog was dangerous. Though the dog had previously scratched another person, the dog had never engaged in an unprovoked attack that caused a serious injury, as contemplated by the statute. As such, the dog is likely not dangerous.

## Step 4 – State Overall Conclusion

Accordingly, because an essential element of the statute is lacking, Mr. Gerardi will not be responsible for paying the medical expenses of the injured child.

The umbrella passage and overall conclusion is where you would maximize on the total points you could earn on the exam. Below is how the analysis of Mr. Gerardi's problem would read if the thesis or umbrella paragraph and IRAC paradigm were pulled together. The labels are purposefully missing and the paragraphs are merged so that you can see how the answer would read in real prose.

According to the relevant dog biting statute, a dog owner is liable for the injuries his dog caused to another if: (1) the dog was dangerous; (2) the dog was not on the owner's real property; and (3) the dog is either unleashed or unmuzzled or both. Mr. Gerardi's dog was not on his property, as he was on public property. Moreover, his dog was neither leashed nor muzzled. Thus, the only disputed issue is whether his dog was dangerous. Though the dog had previously scratched another person, the dog had never engaged in an unprovoked attack that caused a serious injury, as contemplated by the statute. As such, the dog is likely not dangerous. Accordingly, because an essential element of the statute is lacking, Mr. Gerardi will not be responsible to pay the medical expenses of the injured child.

The only[12] disputed issue is whether Mr. Gerardi's dog is dangerous. In deciding whether a dog is dangerous, courts will look at whether the dog has previously injured another person in an unprovoked attack and the extent of those injuries. In the absence of a prior incident resulting in serious injuries caused directly from an attack, a dog that injures another person when unprovoked will not be considered a "dangerous dog" within the meaning of the statute. Moreover, the mere existence of a prior incident in which normal playful dog behavior results in a minor injury to another is not enough to establish dangerousness.

In the *Dog Scratcher* case, the dog at issue had a history of getting excitable around strangers, but had never injured any one before. Thus, the court found that the dog was not dangerous within the meaning of the statute. Similarly, the dog in the *Dog Biter* case was not dangerous. Even though there was a prior incident in which the dog barked and jumped on another person's

---

[12] The word "only" was not in the sample IRAC earlier in the chapter. It was added to the Issue Statement here so that the writing would flow better from the Overall Conclusion in the Thesis to the beginning of the IRAC. Otherwise, the IRAC part of the answer is identical to the IRAC discussed earlier in the chapter.

legs, causing that person to fall and scrape her knees, the injury was so minor and an indirect result of typical dog behavior.

In contrast, in the *Dog Attacker* case, the dog attacked another person 6 months prior to the incident at issue directly causing extensive and serious injury to the persons face and arms. Thus, the court found that the dog was dangerous. Similarly, in the *Killer Dog* case, the dog at issue maimed another person just two years earlier. The testimony revealed that the dog had a "killer instinct." As such, the dog was a dangerous dog, causing the type of injury the statute was intended to protect against.

The prior incident in which Mr. Gerardi's dog injured a stranger does not fit the conditions for dangerousness. The prior incident did not involve an unprovoked attack, but rather a scratch, which is typical of dogs, even gentle ones. Moreover, the incident resulted in a minor injury—a scratch—and not a serious injury, like in *The Killer Dog* and *The Dog Attacker* cases. In other words, Mr. Gerardi's situation is most similar to the facts in *The Dog Biter* case and very distinguishable from the *The Dog Attacker* and *The Killer Dog* cases. Thus, Mr. Gerardi's dog is likely not a "dangerous dog" within the meaning of the statute.

If your question were to raise more than one disputed issue, you would modify your thesis to reflect that fact. Your third step of the thesis would be expanded and you would have two or more IRACs—the same number of IRACs as disputed issues. The IRACs would be stacked one after the other. Simple connection words, like the ones highlighted in the below example, would bridge the thesis sentences and the IRACs themselves. Below is how you would write your thesis and organize your analysis if Mr. Gerardi's question raised a disputed issue over whether the dog was on public property in addition to whether the dog was dangerous. If the dog were on Mr. Gerardi's easement, for example, and not on the public street, this issue might be contested and thus involve an analysis deserving of its own IRAC. The example below shows you where you would put that IRAC and how to connect it to the earlier one; though it sets out the basic structure, it does not include any of the actual analysis, as you would need legal authority to do so.

According to the relevant dog biting statute, a dog owner is liable for the injuries his dog caused to another if: (1) the dog was dangerous; (2) the dog was not on the owner's real property; and (3) the dog is either unleashed or unmuzzled or both. Mr. Gerardi's was neither leashed nor muzzled. Thus, the **two** disputed issues are whether his dog was dangerous and whether he was on public property. Though the dog had previously scratched another person, the dog had never engaged in an unprovoked attack that caused a serious injury, as contemplated by the statute. As such, the dog is likely not dangerous. **However**, the dog was likely on public property because courts routinely consider easements public in nature. **Nonetheless**, because the essential element of dangerousness is lacking, Mr. Gerardi will not be responsible to pay the medical expenses of the injured child.

The **first** disputed issue is whether Mr. Gerardi's dog is dangerous. In deciding whether a dog is dangerous, courts will look at whether the dog has previously injured another person in an unprovoked attack and the extent of those injuries. In the absence of a prior incident resulting in serious injuries caused directly from an attack, a dog that injures another person when unprovoked will not be considered a "dangerous dog" within the meaning of the statute. Moreover, the mere existence of a prior incident in which normal playful dog behavior results in a minor injury to another is not enough to establish dangerousness.

In the *Dog Scratcher* case, the dog at issue had a history of getting excitable around strangers, but had never injured any one before. Thus, the court found that the dog was not dangerous within the meaning of the statute. Similarly, the dog in the *Dog Biter* case was not dangerous. Even though there was a prior incident in which the dog barked and jumped on another person's legs, causing that person to fall and scrape her knees, the injury was so minor and an indirect result of typical dog behavior.

In contrast, in the *Dog Attacker* case, the dog attacked another person 6 months prior to the incident at issue directly causing extensive and serious injury to the persons face and arms. Thus, the court found that the dog was dangerous. Similarly, in the *Killer Dog* case, the dog at issue maimed another person just two years earlier. The testimony revealed that the dog had a "killer instinct." As such, the dog was a dangerous dog, causing the type of injury the statute was intended to protect against.

The prior incident in which Mr. Gerardi's dog injured a stranger does not fit the conditions for dangerousness. The prior incident did not involve an unprovoked attack, but rather a scratch, which is typical of dogs, even gentle ones. Moreover, the incident resulted in a minor injury—a scratch—and not a serious injury, like in *The Killer Dog* and *The Dog Attacker* cases. In other words, Mr. Gerardi's situation is most similar to the facts in *The Dog Biter* case and very distinguishable from the *The Dog Attacker* and *The Killer Dog* cases. Thus, Mr. Gerardi's dog is likely not a "dangerous dog" within the meaning of the statute.

The **second** disputed issue is whether the dog was on public property. [The IRAC would continue with the Rule, Rule Support, Application, Reasoning by Analogy and then Conclusion.]

## Where to Earn Points

When looking at the thesis paragraph in comparison to the text of the IRAC analysis in the answer to Mr. Gerardi's problem, you can see why the majority of the points are earned in your IRAC of a disputed issue, not in the thesis paragraph. Because your answers on disputed issues require the most time, you should begin there—both in your thinking and written analysis. Though the thesis or umbrella paragraph precedes the IRAC analysis in the written answer, it does not need to be written in that order. In fact, you should not write that paragraph first, particularly on an exam where time is limited. You should prioritize your writing to ensure that you earn the most points. Moreover, because much of the thesis or umbrella paragraph is pulled from your IRACs, it is easier to write it last, after you have worked through the entire problem.

You should also notice how the writing in all of the examples in this chapter is very simple. Though many of the opinions in your casebooks are verbose and contain much legal jargon, you should not do the same in your legal writing. Those opinions are often older and do not reflect the current standard of good legal writing. Good legal writing today uses clear, simple language, and plain English. Thus, you should avoid legalese and other empty or wordy expressions at all costs. Not only are they unnecessary, but they often distract the reader and create barriers to understanding your analysis. Some of the more popular, yet superfluous, expressions include: "the aforementioned" or "said" or "based on the facts at hand" or "after applying the legal principles to the present facts it is clear that. . . ." These meaningless expressions can be dropped from your writing altogether; instead begin your sentences with whatever text would have followed them. To ensure that your analysis is understandable and pleasing to the reader, cleanse it of all legal jargon and other unnecessary and distracting words and phrases.

# Chapter 6 Exercise:

Review your analysis of Ms. McDonald's problem from the exercise in Chapter 5. Assume your supervisor has asked you to provide a written summary of your analysis on how a court will likely resolve the case. Use a thesis or umbrella paragraph and the IRAC paradigm to organize your analysis.

# Strategies for Studying for and Taking Exams

As has been repeated throughout this book, law school is about learning how to think like a lawyer. Thus, in testing you, professors will be assessing how well you are able to do the main task of a lawyer: analyzing legal problems. They are interested in more than just your knowledge of relevant legal principles; they are interested in your legal reasoning skills. They want to know that you are able to competently apply a legal rule to a new set of facts. For this reason, your exams— regardless of the subject or type (i.e., closed-book, open-book, take-home)—will likely ask you to analyze a new fact pattern and resolve any issues that it raises. You will be graded on your success in identifying the issues, articulating the rules, and applying those rules appropriately.

If your written answers conform to the IRAC organization, your professors will be able to follow your analysis and award you points in each of these areas. Generally, professors will assign more weight to your rule and application sections than to your issue statements and conclusions. As mentioned in the prior chapter, a correct conclusion is worthless if it is not adequately supported by the law. Your conclusion on undisputed issues and thesis or umbrella paragraphs, while also important, will likely still be worth less than your rule statements and application of the law.

The length and complexity of a fact pattern as well as the number of them on a single exam will obviously vary depending on the course and your professor's preference. A single fact pattern might raise more than one claim or defense and therefore multiple issues. It might also involve more than one party or person or question to answer. Despite these variations, a traditional fact pattern will explain what happened factually and then ask you a legal question. The fact patterns involving Mr. Gerardi, Ms. Levine, and Ms. McDonald in earlier chapters are all good illustrations of what you can expect to see on exams.

# Different Types of Exams

The most traditional law school exam is closed-book, meaning that you are unable to use anything other than your memory to answer the exam questions. Thus, you must know all of the issues the questions might raise as well as the rules needed to solve them. In contrast, in an open-book exam, you are allowed to use outside sources, such as your course outline and casebook, during the exam to answer the questions. For these types of exams, the professor may place limits on the kinds of materials you can use and the extent to which you can annotate them, however. Unlike a closed-book exam, your ability to state the correct legal rules is worth less because presumably those rules can be easily found in the material you bring with you to the exam. Instead, the focus is more on your ability to apply those rules appropriately and support your application with sound reasoning and policy.

To avoid searching aimlessly for a legal rule during an open-book exam, you should prepare your outline and casebook differently than you would if you were using them solely as study materials. For example, you should create a table of contents for your outline, use tabs, and cross-reference pages in the casebook or elsewhere. These tools will allow you to navigate your materials with less effort. You should also consider using complete, grammatical sentences for rules and their explanations so that you can easily plug them into an exam answer. The bottom line is you should be able to use your materials easily and efficiently during the exam.

This is true of take-home exams as well. For these types of exams, you will also be allowed to use outside materials (likely without limitation) to answer the questions. The main difference is the professor will expect your answers to be even more thorough and thoughtful, as well as extremely well-organized and well-written. As a result, take-home exams require that you spend more time outlining, writing, editing, and proofreading your answers than you would normally. Though these types of exams are not traditional in law school, they are becoming more popular, particularly as mid-term assessments, as faculty are now encouraged to give greater feedback to their students throughout the semester.

The only other type of exam is a multiple-choice one. However, it is very unusual to see exclusively multiple-choice exams in law school, particularly in your first-year. It is more common for professors to use multiple-choice questions in combination with traditional fact pattern questions. Nevertheless, multiple-choice questions test the same areas, except that the right answer is there on the page for you to choose. You will still need to employ your legal reasoning skills to choose correctly, though; you will need to know the law, understand it, and apply it. The best way to approach a multiple-choice question is to figure out the answer on your own before reading the choices so that they do not confuse or sidetrack your analysis. Multiple-choice questions can be tricky because many answers seem right, but are, in fact, wrong. Usually they are wrong because they are either incomplete or include partially inaccurate information. Try to eliminate as many wrong answers as you can first and then carefully dissect the remaining choices for completeness and accuracy. Obviously, answer all of the questions, even if you can only make an educated guess, as you do not want to miss out on a chance to earn points.

## Techniques for Memorizing Legal Rules

Though there are many types of exams, the most common one is still a closed-book exam. Therefore, your ability to memorize legal rules so that you can easily recall them on exams is crucial. The best place to start is to study your outline. Use flowcharts, mnemonics, anagrams, images, or catchy phrases to help you remember claims, defenses, elements and other key concepts. As you study, read your outline out loud and review it out of order as well. Because the exam questions will not follow the progression of your outline, you will want to be able to recall concepts without needing the context of your outline to do so. As you internalize the information, try to condense your outline. Eventually, you will want to reduce your outline to a one- or two-page summary of the major doctrinal areas, sub-topics, factual issues, and important cases. You should be able to then look at that condensed outline and fill in the detailed information on your own. Using the skeletal outline as a guide, see if you can write out the expanded version. Re-study the law that was difficult for you to remember or explain and continue to do so until you have fully internalized it.

For visual learners, you can prepare flashcards to review. For auditory learners, try recording key concepts and their explanations in a media format and listening to it repeatedly to reinforce your learning. For kinesthetic learners, who learn best through doing, you can act out the material and, if not possible, simply move around as you work. You can also use study groups to review what you learned. Try teaching your classmates the law; take turns role-playing the "professor" and "student" and mimicking Socratic dialogues that explore answers to hypothetical fact patterns. Whatever it is, find a technique that jives with your learning style and then make it work for you. The key is to be active in your memorization of the law as you collapse your outlines and study for exams.

## Beyond Memorization: Preparing and Studying for the Exam

In addition to learning the doctrine, you will need to practice applying that doctrine to different fact scenarios to ensure that you have not only memorized the material, but also have internalized how to use it. This part of your studying should come after you have comfortably memorized the law. It is an inefficient and unproductive use of your time to attempt to learn the law while simultaneously testing your ability to apply it. Thus, develop a study plan that allots separate and adequate time to both aspects of your studying.

The best way to practice applying the law is to take practice exams. Professors might distribute practice exams or make their old exams available for your review. If either is the case, take advantage of the opportunity to gain insight into how your professor will test you and the chance to analyze fact patterns customized to your course. You might also be able to find good practice questions or hypotheticals in your casebooks or class notes. Though you might also be able to find exam questions elsewhere, such as online or from another professor's course or a commercial study aid, be cautious not to rely too heavily on these outside resources, as they are not adapted in any way to what your professor covered in the course. Once you have exhausted all of the practice exams and preexisting questions, you should work on designing your own exam-like hypotheticals; be sure to consider difficult questions that test all aspects of the law you studied.

Study groups are a perfect place to raise and work out such hypothetical questions. You can compare and debate your answers and critique each other's written analysis, among other things. This outlet can help you identify weaknesses in your analysis (and thus areas to re-study) as well as improve your understanding of the law and its application. If possible, raise the same hypothetical questions with your professors as well to find out whether your analysis of the questions was correct.

You will need to build into your study schedule sufficient time to take practice exams and answer hypothetical exam questions. To ensure that you study at an appropriate pace and are fully prepared by exam time, establish a firm schedule. The schedule should set dates by which important tasks like outlining, memorizing, collapsing the outline, and taking practice exams, should be completed. Make sure you set realistic goals; if your study plan is too ambitious, you will become frustrated and anxious when you miss a goal. You do not want these types of feelings to derail your progress. If you begin studying early, it will be easier to achieve your goals throughout. It will also be much less stressful at the end. A thoughtfully planned schedule should reduce the need to cram or stay up late the night before the exam. Most students perform better when they are well-rested and have an opportunity to let what they studied sink in before taking the exam, even if it is just for one night.

Remember that you do not have to wait until classes are over or your entire outline is complete to move to the next stage of studying. As soon as you complete a topic or section of your casebook or syllabus, you can begin outlining, then memorizing and so on. The material you learn first and last is usually the easiest to recall and apply because the concepts are simple in the beginning and "fresh" in your mind at the end. The material you learn in the middle of the semester, when the concepts become more involved and the exam is still some time away, is often the hardest to study. Thus, you should allot more time to that material as you plan your study schedule.

When it comes time to sit down and study, find a comfortable environment—one that is conducive to your learning needs. For some, it will be a quiet, isolated corner of the library; for others, it will be a busy, loud coffee house. The location itself does not matter as long as you are able to clear it of the things that easily distract you. For many of you, that might mean "disconnecting" from the internet and setting aside the various forms of electronic media that normally consume your day.

## A Quick Detour . . . The Value of Study Groups

Students often question whether there is any real value in working with other students in study groups. Though there are tremendous benefits to collaborative learning, the answer will ultimately depend on what works best for you. For one, study groups are a good way to find out whether you are on the right track, particularly when there are so few opportunities for assessment in law school. Professors have limited availability and cannot provide the type of continuous feedback or ongoing dialogue about the material and its meaning that your classmates can. Additionally, study groups are a good forum for asking questions, clarifying misunderstandings, filling in blanks, analyzing hypotheticals, and practicing exam questions. Because of your shared experience, your classmates can also provide invaluable emotional support and encouragement.

Most of the criticism over study groups relates to personality and productivity issues. As with any group dynamic, if one member is unprepared, there could be a freeloader problem, which inevitably (and justifiably) annoys the prepared students. This problem often results in the unprepared student benefitting from the group's collective hard work even though that student contributed little to nothing to the end product. The group's progress might also be slowed as it waits for the unprepared student to catch up. Additionally, problems arise when one student moves faster or slower than the rest in the group, or when a single member is controlling or overbearing. A group that gets along too well and turns into a social gathering can likewise be unproductive. Needless to say, it is difficult to find the perfect group dynamic—one that has similarly thinking and committed students with personalities that do not clash.

To increase your chances of picking a study group that fits your needs, you should discuss with your classmates what they hope to get out of the process and how they envision collaborating on that effort. This very candid discussion should help you assess early on whether your peers share the same goals as you. If not, look to build relationships with other students in your class that do.

To avoid the problems associated with study groups, establish goals for the group and assign specific tasks that must be completed in order to reach those goals. Example goals might include reading and briefing a set of cases, completing a portion of an outline, writing an answer to a practice exam question, and devising challenging test hypotheticals. You can also establish ground rules for working together. For example, everyone must come to the group having completed the assigned tasks and with written questions and ideas for how to study the material. The ground rules can address other important mechanics as well, like when, how often, and for how long the group will meet, how the group will share information, and whether the group will entertain social or other digressions. A study group that has clear goals and firm ground rules is more likely to have a productive, cooperative, and overall positive experience.

Nevertheless, working in a study group is not essential to your success in law school. Many students find that they can effectively study alone. In fact, some parts of the studying process, such as memorizing the law, outlining, and writing exam answers, should be practiced alone. The question is whether your individual work should be supplemented with group work. Ultimately, you will have to decide whether the benefits of a study group outweigh the costs of investing in one.

## Taking the Exam

As soon as you receive the exam, you should skim through it once to familiarize yourself with the questions and to determine the order in which you will tackle them. During your initial skim, you will want to assess the number, length, and complexity of the questions as well as the general topics they address. You will want to also take into account any point allocation or suggestions your professor has made on the time you should spend on each question. Based on this information, you should develop a plan for how to proceed. You do not need to answer the questions in the order in which they were presented so long as you answer all of the questions. Pick a starting point that will maximize your success on the exam. This might mean beginning with the question that is worth the most to ensure that you have ample time to earn all of the points assigned to it. Alternatively, you could begin with what you perceive to be the easiest question so that you build your confidence early before moving on to the more challenging parts of the exam. After you decide on an order, however, try to stick with it, as you do not want to waste too much time on prioritizing.

Once you begin working on a problem, read the question carefully and skim the fact pattern first before taking any notes or marking up the exam itself. If you do not follow this suggestion and annotate the text immediately, you are likely to focus on information that is irrelevant and miss information that is relevant. The scope of the question and the relevance of certain facts will not be completely apparent until after you have read it through once. During your second read, which you should do more slowly and carefully, you should aim to spot or identify the main issues and precise sub-issues. As you do so, you should take margin notes or highlight or underline the text, as needed.

After identifying the issues, you should begin jotting down information that will help you analyze them, like the relevant rules, pertinent policy, and key words and phrases. If it is helpful to "brain dump" memorized parts of your outline or other information at this point, do so, particularly if it is relevant to the analysis and you are concerned that you will forget it when it comes time to outline and write your answer. For example, if you tend to panic on exams, listing memorized words, issues, names, etc. might be worthwhile to guarantee that you have ideas to jog your memory should your nerves overcome you. You can also "brain dump" earlier during the exam if there is important information you do not think you will be able to retain for very long. Try not to "brain dump" arbitrarily and excessively, though, as you do not want to spend too much time writing down information that might later turn out to be totally unnecessary. Once more, you will need to weigh the time it would take you to "dump" the information against the benefit you will get from seeing it when answering the questions.

Once you have notes on all of the issues, you will need to organize your analysis of them. For each issue, you will need to present a rule, explain the rule, apply it to the facts, and reach a conclusion. Outlining this analysis, using the IRAC paradigm, even if only in a skeletal way, will simplify the writing of your exam answer. Your outline should include a list of all of the facts relevant to the particular issue. In applying the rule to the facts, you will want to use them, not simply restate them. Your goal is to show the reader how they support your conclusion on the issue. You will do this in your written analysis of all of the issues, which, unless directed otherwise, should conform to the IRAC paradigm. Remember to address alternatives or opposing arguments. Though you will want to be objective in your analysis of the facts, you should reach a conclusion and support it persuasively using all of the facts given to you. Do not invent facts or assume facts that are not present in the fact pattern. If you must assume a fact because it is necessary to fill in a gap that would turn the issue one way or the other, explicitly state your assumption for the professor and how it impacts your analysis.

After writing your analysis of all of the disputed issues, make sure that you have explicitly answered your professor's question, which might be broader than any one issue. If it requires that you balance or consider your conclusions on all of the issues, disputed and undisputed ones, do so clearly in an umbrella or thesis paragraph, as described in the prior chapter. Ideally, this paragraph would precede your written analysis on the specific issues; however, in an in-class, timed exam, it might be difficult to write this paragraph first. Therefore, write it last. This paragraph is what will bring your analysis of all of the issues together; it should nicely summarize your answer to the question. If written well, it will likely make the difference between an A and B grade on the exam.

Even if you write this paragraph last, when typing your exam, you can easily cut and paste it to the top of your answer. If you are writing your exam by hand, you can connect the paragraph to the earlier ones by using a transition word or topic sentence that signals your overall conclusion and answer to the professor's question. For example, you might begin with "In Conclusion, because all of the elements of the claim are present, the court will likely find that the plaintiff will prevail in the action." Or "In Conclusion, because one of the necessary elements of the claim is absent, the court will likely find that the plaintiff will not prevail in the action." If necessary to justify your overall conclusion, your subsequent sentences can address your conclusions on the specific elements.

Additionally, you should limit this thesis or umbrella paragraph to answering the question asked. Do not try to impress the professor by talking about non-issues or irrelevant facts. Professors will not award points for your discussion on these topics and might even deduct points for not following directions. At a minimum, your digressions will annoy the professor and you should never set out to annoy the person who will eventually decide your grade.

Finally, if you run out of time, attempt to quickly address any outstanding questions by outlining your answers. You should use the headings for the IRAC paradigm (Issue, Rule, Application, and Conclusion) to save time on writing complete sentences. Under each heading, you can jot down all relevant information that applies. Try to earn as many points as you can by spotting the issues and stating the rules, even if you do not have time to analyze them completely.

## Exam Composition

Though professors might claim that they do not deduct points for poor composition on exams, especially on in-class ones, it undoubtedly factors into your grade, even if only indirectly. An exam answer that fails to use proper syntax, grammar, or spelling or conform to formatting guidelines runs the risk of distracting and irritating the professor. When the professor (or any reader for that matter) is confronted with a writing mistake, he or she is forced to "correct" it to make sense of the text's meaning. With each mistake, the writing becomes less comprehensible and more time-consuming to follow. Writing mistakes can also obscure a writer's original intentions, as any nuances in the use and placement of language are lost as the reader struggles to simply understand the substance of what was written. Also, regardless of whether it is true, professors are apt to assume that a poorly written answer is the product of a lazy and careless writer. Because professors have to spend more time on such answers, they are often more critical of the analysis they put forth and, as a result, harsher in the grading of it.

To ensure that your exam composition does not negatively impact your grade, follow the most basic rules of good writing. First, always use proper grammar and spelling and write in complete sentences with correct punctuation. Do not use private shorthand or abbreviations. If you are using a computer, do not rely solely on the spell check feature to review your document's spelling, as it will not catch wordos and other mistakes. Second, write with clarity and conciseness. Keep sentence and paragraph lengths short. Avoid legal jargon (i.e. "heretofore" and "aforementioned") and pretentious writing ("I opine that. . ."), and strike needless words or phrases (i.e. "after careful consideration, it is clear that . . ."). Humor and sarcasm can often be misunderstood in writing and therefore should also be avoided. Instead, use a conversational, respectful tone, as well as clear and simple language.

Finally, try to organize your analysis around strong topic sentences and conclusions. A good topic sentence will reflect the main idea of the paragraph and a good concluding sentence will complete the idea of the paragraph, not simply restate the topic sentence. Also, use effective transitions—ones that smoothly move the reader from one sentence, paragraph, or idea to the next. If it is helpful, use numbering (i.e., first, second, third, finally) or transition or connector words (i.e., additionally, moreover, however, therefore) to link what you have just said to what will follow. Though you might not be able to devote a whole lot of time to the organization of your writing on the exam, you should strive to break up the analysis into short, distinct paragraphs that are easy to read. A clear, well-written exam answer will please your professor, making him or her more inclined to assign a higher grade.

## After the Exam

Once you have completed an exam, you should try to relax and take a break from law school, even if it is only a short one. See a movie, play a video game, go out to dinner, or socialize with family and friends. It makes no difference what you do, just as long as you spend some time on an activity that is not related to law school. If you take a break with your classmates, avoid talking about the exam and your answers. Doing so will only stress you out. When students try to replay what happened on an exam, they often misremember or confuse the questions and their answers. If you compare what you wrote on the exam with someone else's answers, there is a very good chance that you will share incomplete or inaccurate information. Thus, using that information to evaluate how well you did on the exam is futile. Moreover, you do not really know what your professor expects on the exam or even how your answers match up against your classmates'—an important fact given that most courses are curved. Therefore, you should not waste your time on guesswork, particularly when it has the potential of making you doubt your performance on the exam. Such self-doubt and worry is counterproductive. Once the exam is over, there is nothing you can do to change the outcome, anyway.

Additionally, if you still have exams to take, you need to remain positive about your abilities and stay focused on your future tasks. A break in which you momentarily forget about law school will help you clear your mind of the past and motivate you to continue studying hard for the next exam.

After your last exam of the semester, you should take a real vacation from law school. If you followed this book's instructions on how to succeed, you have worked intensely throughout the semester and thus are deserving of some serious relaxation. You should enjoy your time away from law school, remembering that law school is just a small part of a long life. While grades are important, they should not define who you are, nor prevent you from pursuing your career goals. Good grades might take you to your end goal faster, but they are not the only path to getting there. Experience, determination, and patience will. Therefore, do not lose perspective when it comes to law school grades.

# Chapter 7 Exercise:

Before you begin to study and prepare for law school exams, you should reflect on all aspects of your learning. The following questions will help you assess your individual learning styles and needs. With this information, you can change your study habits and adapt the techniques you use to get ready for exams.

1. Describe the way you best memorize information. Consider whether any of the following techniques are helpful to you: flowcharts or diagrams, anagrams, images or pictures, music, reading quietly, reading out loud, teaching others, flashcards, or physical movement.

2. Describe your ideal environment for reading and studying. Consider the following: location, physical space, noise, and time of day.

3. Explain whether you prefer working alone or collaborating with others.

4. Describe the ground rules you would establish when working in a study group.

5. Describe what you like to do in your free time. Identify an activity that you could do to take a short break from law school in-between exams.

# Staying Afloat: Your Emotional and Psychological Well-being

There can be tremendous pressure in law school. Most everything is new—the subject matter, the "Langdellian" method of teaching, the Socratic questioning, legal writing, the reading, note taking and outlining, exams, as well as the way you are graded. These new experiences can cause heightened anxiety and stress for many students, even for those who traditionally manage pressure well. The social pressures of law school are significant too. Socratic questioning in classes, which are mostly large in the first year, can be uncomfortable for many students. When you are the student "on call," your peers, not just your professor, are able to observe your performance and judge your abilities. Under these circumstances, wrong or inarticulate answers can seem humiliating and sometimes even demoralizing. Thus, the classroom dynamic puts great demand on students to stay competitive with their classmates. The fact that most first-year classes are also subject to a mandatory curve only intensifies the competition, making it hard for students to develop genuine collegial relationships with their classmates.

Moreover, the demands of law school can make it difficult for law students to maintain a personal life outside of school. Therefore, it is not uncommon for students to become totally emerged in their studies, even if just temporarily, at the expense of their relationships with family and non-law school friends. The reality is that your relationships with them provide a much needed outlet and healthy perspective on your law school experience. The less time you spend with them, the more likely you are to feel isolated and alone—feelings that only exacerbate any stress you might already face.

Law school also tends to attract overachievers—students who are accustomed to success, whether it be in their personal life, education or prior employment. Thus, they thrive on the happiness that success brings. Because they expect that they will be equally successful in law school, they can experience great disappointment when that does not happen. The exorbitant cost of a legal education today only intensifies the need to succeed. Even more so than ever, students who enter law school believe that they must graduate at the top of their class in order to obtain a job and pay off their high law school debt. These beliefs can obviously have negative psychological consequences.

## How to Manage the Pressure

A critical part to handling the pressure is maintaining a positive attitude and staying healthy both physically and emotionally. Balancing the personal and work aspects of law school can be challenging, but it is not impossible if you follow some very general principles that underscore the importance of caring for both your mind and body. They include engaging in physical activity, continuing to do the things that matter to you, staying in touch with those who support you, and remembering that law school is just the first small step in a long legal career. These principles, though admittedly basic, are the surest way to manage the many pressures of law school.

Because physical health can have a large influence on mental health, one concrete way to deal with your stress is to exercise regularly. If you exercised before coming to law school, continue to do so, even if you can only do so moderately. For example, if you were an avid runner, take a long run every so often to keep your body in shape and, more importantly, to give your mind a rest. For those of you who did little to no exercise before coming to law school, you should begin exercising for the same reasons. You do not need to dramatically change your lifestyle. But, you should not remain sedentary, either. Leave the library, your apartment, or wherever you study for a couple of hours each week and get moving. For example, take a walk or jog, ride a bike, play tennis, or throw a ball around. By engaging in some sort of physical activity, you will not only improve your physical well-being, but also your mental health, as regular exercise is known to alleviate anxiety and reduce stress. Thus, you should care for your body while in law school.

Additionally, you should stay connected to your family and loved ones and continue your relationships with your non-law school friends. Though you might not be able to talk and visit with them as often as you did before law school, do not lose all contact with them.  They are usually very sympathetic to your situation.  As outsiders, they can also be helpful in reminding you that there is a world beyond law school, where class rank and other markers are insignificant.  They can also provide great opportunities for you to momentarily abandon your law school worries and have fun; time away from your everyday pressures will help you re-energize and be more positive about the work you still have to accomplish.

You should try to find other ways to stay balanced too.  Do not become so caught up in the drudgery of law school that you forget to do the things that you love and make you happy.  If you enjoy reading, then read for fun; read a short novel, a magazine or newspaper.  Take an occasional break to watch a movie, go out to dinner, and pamper yourself.  Also, stay abreast of current events.  Not only will they frequently relate to the work you are doing in law school, but they will also remind you that your law school experience is small relative to what is happening nationally and globally.

At law school, work on building lasting relationships with your classmates, the faculty, and administration.  Join clubs, volunteer, and participate in extracurricular activities.  By focusing on something other than your academics, you will become more integrated into the law school community and less preoccupied and distracted by the academic competition.  You should also form study groups with people you like and with whom you share common interests.  Study groups are not just a useful way to prepare for class and study for exams.  They can also be a great vehicle to vent your concerns and anxieties with people in the same situation as you.

The faculty and administration are another great resource.  The more you get to know them, the more comfortable you will be in soliciting advice on how best to navigate the stress of law school.  If at any point you feel that you are drowning in the pressures and these strategies are not enough, you should seek help from the administration.  Many law schools have established academic support centers or advisors, professional counselors, and other resources on hand.  If you need to consult with someone in a more professional capacity, do not hesitate to do so.

In the end, your happiness and health is the most important part of your success in law school.  While grades are important, they do not and should not define you.  Not everyone will be at the top of the class; it is not even statistically possible. For those who are, it might be easier for them to get a high-paying job or prestigious clerkship. Indeed, good grades and a strong resume is the most direct route to achieving both. However, it is not the only route. Many students will take a less direct path to reach the same goals. Frankly, the route you take to get to your goal will not matter in the long run. Once you are there, no one will care to know how you got there or how long it took. The only thing that really matters is that you are there. Thus, do not put too much significance on the assessments you receive in law school. You will become a lawyer some day and if you are both healthy and happy, you will likely become a very productive and successful one.

# Chapter 8 Exercise:

To help you maintain a balanced law school experience, you should think about your physical, emotional, and psychological well-being. Below is a list of adjectives used often by law students when describing their emotions about law school. These emotions are all very natural and expected. Review the list and identify the ones that best describe how you feel. If you experience feelings that are not mentioned here, you can write them down as well. Once you have defined your emotional state, reflect on what has caused you to have those feelings. If time and resources were not an issue, what would be the best way for you to cope with the negative feelings and focus on the more positive ones? Explain.

Skilled

Stressed

Motivated

Overwhelmed

Proud

Uncertain

Depressed

Happy

Confused

Imbalanced

Tired

Scared

Confident

Alone

Excited

Average

Challenged

# APPENDIX

## Chapter 1 Exercise Answer Key:

1. The issue is whether Travis, the chimpanzee, is a "wild animal" within the meaning of the Connecticut statute.

2.

   a. The issue is an undisputed one because the statute explicitly includes chimpanzees as a type of wild animal.

   b. Because Travis, the chimpanzee, is a "wild animal" within the meaning of the Connecticut statute, his owner, Ms. Herold, is strictly liable for Ms. Nash's injuries.

3.

   a. Stated broadly, the issue is whether Travis, the chimpanzee, has "dangerous propensities" within the meaning of the Connecticut statute. More specifically, the issue is whether a fourteen-year-old chimpanzee who lived and socialized like a human being since infancy and had no prior history of violence has "dangerous propensities" within the meaning of the Connecticut statute where he was acting so rambunctious on the day of the attack that his owner gave him Xanax to relax.

   b. This issue is a disputed one because the meaning of the term "dangerous propensities" is ambiguous.

   c. In order to resolve this issue, the student must first find the relevant law. The student must read Connecticut cases that address this issue to synthesize a legal rule for the term "dangerous propensities." Once the student has a legal rule, he or she can apply it to the facts to reach a decision.

d. There is a good argument that Travis does not have "dangerous propensities" as he lived his entire life in a socialized, non-violent, manner. Though chimpanzees can be aggressive as they reach adulthood, other than the incident in question, Travis exhibited no such aggression. To the contrary, during his one prior escape, he was playful as he held up traffic. His ability to perform on television, be photographed, and eat, drink, dress, and bathe himself as a responsible human being belies any argument that he was dangerous.

There is also a good argument that Travis has "dangerous propensities." Despite his ability to socialize and perform many of the functions that a responsible human being does, he is nonetheless a wild animal. Chimpanzees, by their very nature, have astonishing power and an adult male like Travis has the upper body strength that exceeds that of an adult human by 4 – 5 times. Moreover, as adults, they are known to act aggressively toward their owners. Though Travis had no prior history of violence, he did have a history of escape and, on the day of the incident, was acting so rambunctious that his owner had to give him Xanax to relax.

4.

a. Below is a chart of the cases:

| Case Name | Facts | Holding "dangerous propensities"? | Reasoning |
|---|---|---|---|
| The Bearded Dragon Lizard | Bearded dragon lizard nipped Plaintiff's finger causing injuries | No | Though fearsome-looking when beard is puffed, it is gentle-spirited; adapts well to |

| | | | |
|---|---|:---:|---|
| | | | humans and enjoys their company; other than occasional bite when feeding, this lizard is not naturally aggressive or harmful at any age |
| The Lion Cub | Lion cub bit Plaintiff several times on leg; Plaintiff needed 30+ stitches for her injuries; lion cub raised like baby, feeding, bathing and cuddling like one of Defendant's children | ✓ | Though lion cubs are tame in their infancy, they are wild animals. As such, with age, they become aggressive in captivity. It is instinctive for them to bite and their bite can be very dangerous. |
| The Gator | Pet alligator, which was 4 ½ feet in length and weighed approx. 180 lbs, escaped from Defendant's property and viscously attacked Plaintiff-neighbor. Plaintiff's injuries to face, hands, arms, and legs were serious. | ✓ | Alligators are wild animals; by their very nature, they are dangerous, ferocious animals. Even in infancy, they can attack. As adults, they will treat any animal— human or otherwise—that nears them as prey. They eat wild boars, deer, dogs, and even livestock. There is no question that they are dangerous and thus should not be kept as pets. |

b.  In deciding whether an animal has "dangerous propensities," Connecticut courts consider whether the animal is a wild animal and whether it exhibits naturally aggressive or harmful behavior. The fact that a wild animal might be tame in its infancy does not seem to matter if that animal, as an adult, is typically aggressive. Thus, an aggressive animal that has an instinct to bite (i.e. lion cub) and prey on other animals (i.e. alligator) has "dangerous propensities" within the meaning of the Connecticut statute. On the other hand, an animal that is gentle-spirited and not naturally aggressive or harmful at any age (i.e. lizard) does not have "dangerous propensities" within the meaning of the Connecticut statute even if that animal occasionally bites while feeding.

c.  A court will likely find that Travis has "dangerous propensities" within the meaning of the Connecticut statute. Chimpanzees are wild animals and thus naturally very powerful and dangerous animals. Though pet chimpanzees might be tame in their infancy and capable of exhibiting many human traits and behaviors, much like the lion cub, they typically act aggressively toward their owners when they reach adulthood. This aggression, like the aggression lion cubs show as they age in captivity, can be very dangerous, as they possess astonishing power. For example, the average adult male has 4 - 5 times the upper body strength of an adult human. The ability to use this strength to harm a human that it perceives as a threat is as instinctive as the lion cub's bite or the alligator's desire to attack prey that nears it. Though Travis might have adapted well to humans for a good period of his life, unlike the bearded lizard, which is always gentle-spirited and not harmful or dangerous at any age, chimpanzees do become aggressive as adults, particularly when kept as pets, as Travis was.

d.  Because Travis likely has "dangerous propensities" within the meaning of the Connecticut statute, strict liability applies. As such, Ms. Herold, as his owner, will be liable to pay for the injuries Travis caused to Ms. Nash.

# Chapter 2 Exercise Answer Key:

1. Below is the annotation in table format for the *Illian* decision.

| | |
|---|---|
| 66 A.D.3d 1312, 888 N.Y.S.2d 247 | Citation |
| Supreme Court, Appellate Division, Third Department, New York.<br>Ann ILLIAN et al., Appellants,<br>v.<br>Gail BUTLER et al., Respondents.<br><br>Oct. 29, 2009. | Caption |
| GARRY, J. | Authoring Judge |
| Appeal from an order of the Supreme Court (Cahill, J.), entered July 11, 2008 in Ulster County, which granted defendants' motion for summary judgment dismissing the complaint. | Procedural History |
| In June 2005, while plaintiffs were temporarily residing at a campground in Accord, Ulster County, plaintiff Ann Illian (hereinafter plaintiff) was bitten by Sadie, a mixed-breed dog belonging to defendants, who also resided at the campground. Defendants and plaintiffs had known one another for years, and plaintiff was also well acquainted with the dog. Plaintiff testified that she had patted Sadie, played with her, and kissed her on numerous prior occasions without incident, and had once even taken her to the veterinarian. On the day of plaintiff's injury, she attended a party at defendants' campground residence to celebrate defendant Jeffrey Sloat's birthday. During the party, Sadie was tied by a chain on defendants' front porch, where plaintiff patted her once or twice in the course of the evening. Shortly before she was bitten, plaintiff left defendants' residence briefly. Upon her return, she reached out to pat Sadie as she climbed | Relevant and Background facts |

| | |
|---|---|
| the porch steps. The dog lunged and bit plaintiff in the face. | |
| Plaintiff and her husband, derivatively, commenced this action in May 2007. Defendants moved for summary judgment dismissing the complaint, contending that they neither knew nor should have known of the dog's vicious propensities. Supreme Court granted defendants' motion. | Procedural History |
| Plaintiffs now appeal. | Procedural Posture |
| "[A] plaintiff may not recover for injuries sustained in an attack by a dog unless he or she establishes that the dog had vicious propensities and that its owner knew or should have known of such propensities'" (*Malpezzi v. Ryan,* 28 A.D.3d 1036, 1037, 815 N.Y.S.2d 295 (2006), quoting *Palleschi v. Granger,* 13 A.D.3d 871, 872, 786 N.Y.S.2d 627 (2004); *see Collier v. Zambito,* 1 N.Y.3d 444, 446, 775 N.Y.S.2d 205, 807 N.E.2d 254 (2004)). The owner's knowledge may be established by proving that the owner had notice of either a prior bite or other conduct that would give rise to an inference of vicious propensities (*see Collier v. Zambito,* 1 N.Y.3d at 446-447, 775 N.Y.S.2d 205, 807 N.E.2d 254). "[E]vidence that the dog 'had been known to growl, snap or bare its teeth' might be enough to raise a question of fact, depending on the circumstances" (*Brooks v. Parshall,* 25 A.D.3d 853, 853-854, 806 N.Y.S.2d 796 (2006), quoting *Collier v. Zambito,* 1 N.Y.3d at 447, 775 N.Y.S.2d 205, 807 N.E.2d 254). Once knowledge of a dog's vicious propensities has been established, the owner faces strict liability (*see Bard v. Jahnke,* 6 N.Y.3d 592, 596-597, 815 N.Y.S.2d 16, 848 N.E.2d 463 (2006); *Collier v. Zambito,* 1 N.Y.3d at 448, 775 N.Y.S.2d 205, 807 N.E.2d 254). | Applicable Law (precedent rules) |

| | |
|---|---|
| Defendants supported their motion for summary judgment with their own testimony that Sadie, whom they had owned since she was five weeks old, had never previously bitten anyone and that they had never seen her behave aggressively nor received complaints from anyone about her behavior. In addition, they submitted plaintiffs' testimony that, in numerous previous interactions with Sadie, they had not known her to bite or threaten anyone and had never expressed concern about her to defendants (*see* CPLR 3212(b); *Rose v. Heaton,* 39 A.D.3d 937, 938, 833 N.Y.S.2d 291 (2007); *Campo v. Holland,* 32 A.D.3d 630, 631, 820 N.Y.S.2d 352 (2006); *Brooks v. Parshall,* 25 A.D.3d at 854, 806 N.Y.S.2d 796)). | Relevant facts |
| This evidence was sufficient to shift the burden to plaintiffs to establish the existence of triable issues of fact (*see Zuckerman v. City of New York,* 49 N.Y.2d 557, 562, 427 N.Y.S.2d 595, 404 N.E.2d 718 (1980)).<br><br>Plaintiffs' evidence was insufficient to meet their burden (*see id.*), particularly in light of their own longstanding familiarity with the dog. | Issue, Holding and Reasoning |
| Plaintiffs submitted the testimony of defendants' former neighbor that Sadie barked, jumped, and ran onto the neighbor's campsite when she and her husband drove in. The campground activities director testified that on one occasion the dog frightened her by leaping off the porch, barking, and running toward her as she walked past. Neither witness had made any complaint to defendants regarding the dog's behavior. | Relevant facts |
| Further, these observations merely reveal "typical territorial behavior," insufficient to establish vicious | Reasoning<br>(application of precedent rules) |

| | |
|---|---|
| propensities (*Blackstone v. Hayward,* 304 A.D.2d 941, 941-942, 757 N.Y.S.2d 160 (2003), *lv. denied* 100 N.Y.2d 511, 766 N.Y.S.2d 164, 798 N.E.2d 348 (2003); *see Campo v. Holland,* 32 A.D.3d at 631, 820 N.Y.S.2d 352; *Fontanas v. Wilson,* 300 A.D.2d 808, 808-809, 751 N.Y.S.2d 656 (2002)). | |
| Plaintiffs also submitted the testimony of plaintiff's sister and the affidavit of the sister's husband that, about a month before plaintiff was bitten, Sadie growled at the husband. | Relevant facts |
| A single incident of growling does not, however, establish that a dog has vicious propensities (*see Rose v. Heaton,* 39 A.D.3d at 938, 833 N.Y.S.2d 291; *Brooks v. Parshall,* 25 A.D.3d at 854, 806 N.Y.S.2d 796). | Reasoning (application of precedent rules) |
| Further, the husband could not confirm that either of the defendants was present during this incident, and neither he nor the sister alleged that they told defendants about it. | Relevant facts |
| Finally, as the campground required all dogs to be leashed, the fact that defendants kept Sadie tethered does not indicate any knowledge of the alleged vicious propensities (*see Collier v. Zambito,* 1 N.Y.3d at 447, 775 N.Y.S.2d 205, 807 N.E.2d 254). While witness testimony contradicting an owner's claims relative to a dog's conduct may be sufficient to establish issues of fact as to credibility or the owner's constructive knowledge, the proof presented here does not rise to that level (*see Loper v. Dennie,* 24 A.D.3d 1131, 1133, 807 N.Y.S.2d 672 (2005); *Czarnecki v. Welch,* 13 A.D.3d 952, 953, 786 N.Y.S.2d 659 (2004)). | Relevant facts & Reasoning (application of precedent rules) |
| Defendants were therefore entitled to | Holding |

| | |
|---|---|
| summary judgment dismissing the complaint. | |
| ORDERED that the order is affirmed, with costs. | Disposition |
| ROSE, J.P., STEIN and McCARTHY, JJ., concur. | Concurring Judges |

2. Below is the annotation in table format for the *Malpezzi* decision.

| | |
|---|---|
| 28 A.D.3d 1036, 815 N.Y.S.2d 295 | Citation |
| Supreme Court, Appellate Division, Third Department, New York.<br>Linda MALPEZZI, Individually and as Parent and Guardian of Casey L. Malpezzi, an Infant, Respondent,<br>v.<br>Dennis RYAN, Appellant.<br><br>April 27, 2006. | Caption |
| CREW III, J.P. | Authoring Judge |
| Appeal from an order of the Supreme Court (Hoye, J.), entered June 6, 2005 in Schenectady County, which denied defendant's motion for summary judgment dismissing the complaint. | Procedural History |
| In July 2001, defendant awoke to the sound of a dog crying and discovered "Oreo" caught beneath the picnic table of his neighbor, Gerardo Masi. Defendant and Masi freed the dog and, when Oreo continued to linger on and around defendant's property, defendant contacted the local animal control officer, Rodney Hubert. According to defendant, Hubert opined that the dog, a pit bull, probably had been "dumped" because he "wasn't a fighter" and indicated that if he took the dog in, Oreo either would be claimed by someone who would try to train him to fight or he would be | Background facts |

| | |
|---|---|
| euthanized. As a result, defendant decided to keep Oreo and attempt to find him a home and, following Hubert's advice, contacted the local health department to ascertain whether Oreo had "a record," placed an ad in the local paper and took Oreo to a veterinarian to have him examined and vaccinated. Having received a clean bill of health from both the veterinarian and the health department, defendant took Oreo home, purchased a leash, collar and harness and set up a place for Oreo in the shed in his back yard. | |
| Over the course of the next two months, Oreo interacted with defendant, his girlfriend and their children without incident. Notably, defendant testified at his examination before trial that at no point during this time period did Oreo bark, growl or bare his teeth at, jump on or display any aggression toward any person or animal. | Relevant facts |
| On the evening of September 14, 2001, defendant and his family, as was their custom, took Oreo for a walk along a local bike path where they ultimately encountered Casey Malpezzi, then six years old, and his brother, Michael. Although there is some dispute as to what then transpired, there is no question that Oreo bit Malpezzi on the arm | Relevant facts and Background |
| and, as a result, plaintiff thereafter commenced this action against defendant seeking to recover for the injuries Malpezzi sustained. Following joinder of issue and discovery, defendant moved for summary judgment dismissing the complaint. Supreme Court denied that motion, finding a question of fact as to whether defendant was aware of Oreo's allegedly vicious propensities. | Procedural History |

| | |
|---|---|
| This appeal by defendant ensued. | Procedural Posture |
| We reverse and grant defendant's motion for summary judgment dismissing the complaint. | Disposition |
| As this Court consistently has held, "a plaintiff may not recover for injuries sustained in an attack by a dog unless he or she establishes that the dog had vicious propensities and that its owner knew or should have known of such propensities" (*Palleschi v. Granger,* 13 A.D.3d 871, 872, 786 N.Y.S.2d 627 (2004); *see Brooks v. Parshall,* 25 A.D.3d 853, 853-854, 806 N.Y.S.2d 796 (2006); *Morse v. Colombo,* 8 A.D.3d 808, 777 N.Y.S.2d 824 (2004)). | Applicable Law (precedent rule) |
| Here, defendant and his girlfriend testified, without contradiction, that they did not experience any problems with the dog prior to the incident with Malpezzi. Specifically, each testified that Oreo did not display any act of aggression prior to biting Malpezzi; Oreo did not bark, growl, bare his teeth or snap at, jump on or chase any person or animal, nor did they receive any complaints from anyone in the neighborhood. Such proof, in our view, is more than adequate to discharge defendant's initial burden on the motion for summary judgment, thereby compelling plaintiff to come forward with sufficient admissible proof to raise a question of fact in this regard. This plaintiff failed to do so. | Issue, Holding and Reasoning |
| In opposition, plaintiff primarily relies upon the purportedly vicious nature of the attack, the fact that Oreo allegedly was restrained while on defendant's property and Oreo's specific breed. | Relevant facts |
| As a starting point, even assuming that Oreo bit Malpezzi on the arm without provocation and in the manner alleged | Reasoning (application of precedent rules) |

| | |
|---|---|
| by plaintiff, that alone is not sufficient to raise a question of fact as to vicious propensities. | |
| Additionally, again assuming that Oreo was chained while on defendant's property-an allegation that defendant disputes-"nothing in our case law suggests that the mere fact that a dog was kept enclosed or chained ... is sufficient to raise a triable issue of fact as to whether it had vicious propensities" (*Collier v. Zambito,* 1 N.Y.3d 444, 447, 775 N.Y.S.2d 205, 807 N.E.2d 254 (2004); *see Palleschi v. Granger, supra* at 872, 786 N.Y.S.2d 627; *Hagadorn-Garmely v. Jones,* 295 A.D.2d 801, 744 N.Y.S.2d 538 (2002)). | Relevant facts & Reasoning (application of precedent rules) |
| Finally, this Court repeatedly has held that "breed alone is insufficient to raise a question of fact as to vicious propensities" (*Palleschi v. Granger, supra* at 872, 786 N.Y.S.2d 627; *see Loper v. Dennie,* 24 A.D.3d 1131, 1133, 807 N.Y.S.2d 672 (2005); *Bard v. Jahnke,* 16 A.D.3d 896, 897, 791 N.Y.S.2d 694 (2005), *lv. granted* 5 N.Y.3d 708, 803 N.Y.S.2d 28, 836 N.E.2d 1151 (2005); *Mulhern v. Chai Mgt.,* 309 A.D.2d 995, 997, 765 N.Y.S.2d 694 (2003), *lv. denied* 1 N.Y.3d 508, 777 N.Y.S.2d 17, 808 N.E.2d 1276 (2004)), and we once again state that "there is no persuasive authority for the proposition that a court should take judicial notice of the ferocity of any particular type or breed of domestic animal" (*Roupp v. Conrad,* 287 A.D.2d 937, 938, 731 N.Y.S.2d 545 (2001)). Simply put, where, as here, there is no other evidence even suggesting that defendant knew or should have known of Oreo's allegedly vicious propensities, consideration of the dog's breed is irrelevant. | Reasoning (application of precedent rules) |
| As such, Supreme Court erred in | Holding |

| denying defendant's motion for summary judgment dismissing the complaint. | |
|---|---|
| ORDERED that the order is reversed, on the law, with costs, motion granted, summary judgment awarded to defendant and complaint dismissed. | Disposition |
| MUGGLIN, ROSE, LAHTINEN and KANE, JJ., concur. | Concurring Judges |

# Chapter 3 Exercise Answer Key:

Below is the complete case brief of the *Illian* decision.

## ILLIAN

New York Appellate Division, 3d Dep't, 2009, p. 40

## Facts:

- Injured person = acquaintance of dog owners; they knew each other for years
- Acquaintance also well acquainted with dog: patted her, played with her, kissed her often, and took to veterinarian once
- Dog a mixed-breed
- On day of injury, dog was tied by chain on owner's front porch of campground residence
- Campground required that all dogs be leashed
- Acquaintance patted dog once or twice earlier that day w/o incident
- Acquaintance left dog owner's residence briefly; upon her return, she reached out to pat dog and dog lunged and bit her on the face
- Dog owners testified that they owned dog since she was 5 weeks old; the dog had never bitten anyone, never acted aggressively, and they never received any complaints about the dog's behavior
- Neighbor testified that dog barked, jumped, and ran onto neighbor's property when she and husband drove in
- Campsite director testified that the dog frightened her by leaping off the porch, barking and running toward her as she walked past
- Dog growled at acquaintance's brother-in-law one month before incident
- No complaints about the dog's behavior were ever lodged by neighbor, director or acquaintance's brother-in-law

**Procedure:**

- NY Supreme Court granted D dog owner's motion for summary judgment (SJ) dismissing complaint
- Injured P (& her husband) appeals

SJ Motion = request that court decide the case (or a portion of it) without a full trial. To prevail, the moving party must establish that there are no issues of material fact requiring a trial and that in applying the law to the undisputed facts the moving party is clearly entitled to judgment in its favor.

**Issue:**

Whether P demonstrated a triable issue of material fact that the mixed-breed dog had vicious propensities and D owner knew or should have known of them where the dog was family pet since she was 5 weeks old and had never bitten anyone before and the owners had never received any complaints about the dog's behavior, but recently the dog had barked, jumped and growled at several people.

**Applicable Law:**

- Court cites New York Court of Appeals decisions but relies mainly on New York Appellate Division cases

- *Malpezzi* (2006) and *Collier* (2004) cited for General Rule that dog owner is liable for injuries caused by his or her dog when the dog has vicious propensities and the owner knew or should have known of such propensities

- Specific Rule for vicious propensities: may include evidence that dog has been known to growl, snap or bare its teeth; single instance of growling not enough though

- Specific Rule for knowledge of propensities: evidence that owner had notice of prior bite or conduct that would give rise to an inference of vicious propensities

**Holding:**

No. There is insufficient evidence that the dog had vicious propensities or that the defendant owner knew or should have known of such propensities.

**Rationale:**

- Testimony by neighbor and campsite director about dog's recent behavior indicative of "typical territorial behavior" and thus is not sufficient to raise triable issue of fact

- Single instance of growling, as alleged by acquaintance's brother-in-law, is also insufficient to establish vicious propensities

- The dog was restrained b/c of camp rule and thus does not indicate any knowledge of vicious propensities

**Rule:**

Specific Rule on Vicious Propensities: Evidence that a dog barks, jumps, or runs after passersby or cars is insufficient to raise a triable issue of fact in the absence of any other evidence of aggressive behavior by the dog. A single instance of a dog growling is not sufficient.

Specific Rule on Knowledge: Evidence that a dog owner restrains a dog because a rule requires that owner do so does not in any way prove knowledge of vicious propensities. Evidence that owner had notice of prior bite or conduct that would give rise to an inference of vicious propensities is sufficient to establish knowledge of such propensities.

**Synthesis:**

Same as in *Miletich* decision case brief.

**Misc.:**

The complaint was properly dismissed. The Court affirmed the lower court's decision.

Below is the complete case brief of the *Malpezzi* decision.

## MALPEZZI

New York Appellate Division, 3d Dep't, 2006, p. 44

**Facts:**

- Dog was an abandoned pit bull that D rescued
- D owner believed that dog might have been dumped b/c he wasn't a "fighter"
- For 2 months, dog interacted with D dog owner, his girlfriend and their children w/o incident
- During that period, dog did not bark, growl or bare his teeth at, jump on or chase any person or animal or display any aggression toward anyone
- During that period, D dog owner did not receive any complaints from anyone in the neighborhood about the dog
- Parties dispute whether dog was chained on D's property
- While D owner was walking dog one day, he bit 6-yr-old P on his arm w/o provocation

**Procedure:**

- NY Supreme Ct denied D dog owner's motion for summary judgment (SJ) dismissing complaint
- D dog owner appeals

**Issue:**

Whether P demonstrated a triable issue of material fact that the pit bull dog had vicious propensities and D owner knew or should have known of them where the pit bull was rescued by D owner after the dog was abandoned and D owned the dog for 2 months, during which time the dog did not exhibit any aggressive behavior and the owner received no complaints, but where the dog bit a 6-year-old boy without provocation.

**Applicable Law:**

- Other than citing one New York Court of Appeals decision (*Collier*), the Court relies on New York Appellate Division cases

- General Rule that dog owner is liable for injuries caused by his or her dog when the dog has vicious propensities and the owner knew or should have known of such propensities

**Holding:**

No. There is insufficient evidence that the dog had vicious propensities or that the defendant owner knew or should have known of such propensities.

**Rationale:**

- The nature of the attack, which lacked provocation, alone is not sufficient to raise a question of fact as to dog's vicious propensities

- Neither is the sole fact that dog was chained on property sufficient to raise a question of fact as to dog's vicious propensities

- Nor is the breed alone sufficient to raise a question of fact as to dog's vicious propensities; because there was no other evidence suggesting that the dog was vicious, the Court cannot consider the breed

**Rule:**

Specific Rules on Vicious Propensities:

1. The breed alone is not sufficient to demonstrate vicious propensities, though it may be considered w/ other factors.

2. Though the manner in which a plaintiff was injured is relevant in deciding whether a dog has vicious propensities, it alone is insufficient.

3. Evidence that a dog owner restrains his or her dog without more is insufficient to demonstrate vicious propensities.

**Synthesis:**

None. First case on this topic.

Specific Rule on Knowledge: Evidence that owner had notice of prior bite or conduct that would give rise to an inference of vicious propensities is sufficient to establish knowledge of such propensities.

**Misc.:**

The Court reversed the lower court's decision and dismissed the complaint.

# Chapter 4 Exercise Answer Key:

Below is an example of one way you could have organized the sub-topic Assault in the Torts Outline, keeping consistent with the organization for the sub-topic Battery in this chapter.

## Torts Outline

- Intentional Acts
- Assault= Actor intended to put someone in apprehension of an immediate harmful or offensive contact.
    - o Reasoning: While battery requires a harmful or offensive contact, assault merely requires apprehension that a harmful or offensive contact is about to occur.
        - ▪ Intent:
            - Specific intent—Actor intends to cause the apprehension of harmful or offensive contact in the victim
                - o Example: D intended to swing arm at P (Case A)
                - o OR
            - General intent—Actor intends to do the act that causes such apprehension
                - o Example: D intended to throw rock in stream, even though D did not aim at or intend to scare P, who ducked to miss being hit by rock (Case B)
        - ▪ Apprehension: Must produce apprehension in the mind of a reasonable person. It will depend on circumstances; it might take less time to create apprehension in mind of child than adult

- Reasonable: Throw rock at someone and miss (Case C)
- Not Reasonable: Clench fist to throw punch at victim, but victim sleeping (Case D); Blow bubbles in someone's direction (hypo)

- <u>Immediate</u> Harmful or Offensive Contact: The threat must be imminent; it must be impending or about to occur.
  - Immediate: Point gun in victim's direction (immediate); throw punch at victim and miss (hypo)
  - Not Immediate: Threaten to kill person 5 years from now (hypo)

- Battery

- Negligence

- Strict Liability

# Chapter 5 Exercise Answer Key:

1. The undisputed elements are: whether the landlord had notice that a dog was being harbored on the premises; and whether the landlord had sufficient control of the premises to allow the landlord to remove or confine the dog. Though she was unsure what type of dog her tenant had, the landlord knew that the tenant had a dog on the property. She saw it on the property and later instructed her tenant to leash it. The landlord did not have the requisite control over the property because she visited it infrequently, only to collect rent and perform maintenance on it.

2. The disputed element is whether the landlord knew or should have known that the dog had vicious propensities.

3. The synthesized rule for whether the landlord knew or should have known that the dog had vicious propensities can be stated as follows:

An absentee landlord who had little to no contact with the offending dog is not likely to be charged with knowledge unless the landlord was made aware of the dog's vicious propensities through direct observation or by others. (*Smedley*) The landlord needs to have personally witnessed the dog acting aggressively (i.e. loud barking, lunging at people) or received complaints to that effect to have knowledge of the dog's vicious propensities. (*Champ-Doran*) A landlord's contact with the dog that is uneventful weighs against having the required knowledge. (*Orozco; Sarno*) Courts are not inclined to impute knowledge to a landlord when the only evidence of viciousness is that the dog growls on occasion or the owner has restrained the dog out of some duty. (*Orozco*) The rule is so pro-landlord that courts will not impute knowledge even when there is evidence of a prior injury by the dog in a public report so long as the landlord was unaware of the injury and corresponding report. (*Georgianna*)

4. Ms. McDonald did not have the requisite knowledge of the dog's vicious propensities. Though there is evidence that the dog had vicious propensities, Ms. McDonald was never made aware of that evidence. (*Smedley*) As an absentee landlord, Ms. McDonald had little contact with the dog. Moreover, whatever contact she had with the dog was uneventful. (*Orozco; Sarno*) Other than the dog's growling at her once or twice before as she approached the house, the dog was always very quiet and even-tempered. She never witnessed the dog acting aggressively toward her or others. (*Champ-Doran*)

Nor had Ms. McDonald ever received any complaints about the dog's aggressiveness from the other tenant or anyone else. (*Champ-Doran*) Though the other tenant complained that she did not like dogs and was afraid of them generally, she never reported any incidences of aggressiveness on the part of Mr. Fox's dog. The fact that the dog was chained while outside, standing alone, is insufficient to impute knowledge, particularly when it was Ms. McDonald who asked Mr. Fox to do so out of respect for the other tenant, not out of fear of the dog's behavior. (*Orozco*)

Moreover, the mere existence of an article in the town paper reporting on a prior incident involving Mr. Fox's dog is insufficient to charge Ms. McDonald with constructive knowledge because an ordinarily prudent person would not scan local newspapers to check on whether a tenant's dog had acted viciously before. (*Georgianna*) Imposing that burden on a landlord would be both "oppressive and unreasonable." (*Georgianna*) Therefore, Ms. McDonald did not have the requisite knowledge.

5. A court will likely find that Ms. McDonald neither knew nor should have known that the dog had vicious propensities.

6. Because Mr. Vitello will be unable to establish two of the three necessary elements of his claim, Ms. McDonald will most likely not be liable for the injuries.

# Chapter 6 Exercise Answer Key:

## Thesis/Umbrella Paragraphs

A plaintiff must establish three elements to recover against an absentee landlord on a theory of strict liability: (1) the landlord had notice that a dog was being harbored on the premises; (2) the landlord knew or should have known that the dog had vicious propensities; and (3) the landlord had sufficient control of the premises to allow the landlord to remove or confine the dog. (*Sarno*)

Elements 1 and 3 are undisputed. Ms. McDonald had notice that the dog was on her property because she saw the dog and spoke to Mr. Fox about leashing it. Though she had notice of the dog, she did not have sufficient control of the premises to remove or confine the dog because she was an absentee landlord. Like in *Sarno*, she visited the property infrequently, only to collect rent and take care of any maintenance issues. Mr. Vitello will likely be unable to prove the remaining disputed element of his claim too. Although there is evidence that the dog had vicious propensities, Ms. McDonald was never made aware of that evidence. Accordingly, because Mr. Vitello will be unable to establish two of the three necessary elements of his claim, Ms. McDonald will most likely not be liable for the injuries.

## Issue

Mr. Vitello will likely be unable to prove that Ms. McDonald knew or should have known of the dog's vicious propensities.

## Rule & Rule Explanation

An absentee landlord who had little to no contact with the offending dog is not likely to be charged with knowledge unless the landlord was made aware of the dog's vicious propensities through direct observation or by others. (*Smedley*) The landlord needs to have personally witnessed the dog acting aggressively (i.e. loud barking, lunging at people) or received complaints to that effect to have knowledge of the dog's vicious propensities. (*Champ-Doran*) A landlord's contact with the dog that is uneventful weighs against having the required knowledge. (*Orozco; Sarno*) Courts are not inclined to impute knowledge to a landlord when the only evidence of viciousness is that the dog growls on occasion or the owner has restrained the dog out of some duty. (*Orozco*)  The rule is so pro-landlord that courts will not impute knowledge even when there is evidence of a prior injury by the dog in a public report so long as the landlord was unaware of the injury and corresponding report. (*Georgianna*)

For example, in *Sarno*, the court held that the landlord did not have the requisite knowledge that the dog, a bull mastiff, had vicious propensities.  The defendants—a husband and wife—were absentee landlords.  The husband visited the property approximately once a month to collect rent and check on the house in general.  On two occasions, he observed a bull mastiff on the property and, on at least one of those occasions he petted the dog on the head without incident.  However, it is unknown whether the dog he observed was the same one that injured the infant plaintiff because the tenants owned two bull mastiffs at the time.  The wife, on the other hand, never noticed any dogs during her visits to the property.

In *Orozco*, the landlord also did not have knowledge that the tenant's dog had vicious propensities despite the fact that other tenants in the building were frightened of the pit bull and it had growled at the superintendent the day before the attack.  The superintendent had never received complaints about the dog and never observed it acting aggressively.  In fact, during his own encounters with the dog in the hallway, the dog passed him "at ease."  The fact that the tenant allegedly tied the dog when it was in the apartment had no bearing since there was no evidence he did so out of fear that his dog would attack someone.

Similarly, in *Smedley*, the landlord did not have knowledge that the tenant's pit bull had any vicious propensities.  The landlord was an absentee landlord in the truest sense; he visited the property at most once a year.  And, even though his neighbors might have been aware that the dog was vicious, he did not know that the dog was even present on the property and he never received any complaints about the dog from the neighbors.  Moreover, the presence of a "Beware of Dog" sign, by itself, was insufficient to impute the landlord with notice of the dog's vicious propensities.

Finally, in *Georgianna*, the court held that the landlord did not have constructive knowledge of her tenant's dog's vicious propensities.  The dog had previously bitten someone and a report of that incident had been filed with the town and county health department.  Though the report may have been publicly available, the court found that there was no duty to inquire about the dog.  The landlord knew the tenant had a dog, but no more.  To create a duty to inquire further would be an oppressive and unreasonable burden in this situation.

However, in *Champ-Doran*, the landlord had the requisite knowledge.  He knew of at least one of the tenant's two dogs and had received complaints from neighbors about the dogs' loud barking and lunging at people through holes in the fence on the property.  He also knew that one of the dogs had previously escaped. By his own testimony, he was aware of the holes in the fence, but claimed he "didn't think any dog could get under" the fence.  He had even previously warned the tenant that the "dogs had to go."  Therefore, he had sufficient knowledge that the dogs at issue had vicious propensities.

## Application & Reasoning by Analogy

Though there is evidence that the dog had vicious propensities, Ms. McDonald was never made aware of that evidence. (*Smedley*)  As an absentee landlord, Ms. McDonald had little contact with the dog.  Moreover, whatever contact she had with the dog was uneventful. (*Orozco; Sarno*)  Other than the dog's growling at her once or twice before as she approached the house, the dog was always very quiet and even-tempered.  She never witnessed the dog acting aggressively toward her or others.

Nor had Ms. McDonald ever received any complaints about the dog's aggressiveness from the other tenant or anyone else.  This is unlike the landlord in *Champ-Doran,* who received complaints about the dog barking and lunging at holes in the property's fence from several neighbors, creating an issue of fact as to his knowledge.  Though Ms. McDonald's other tenant complained that she did not like dogs and was afraid of them generally, she never reported any incidences of aggressiveness on the part of Mr. Fox's dog.  Further, the fact that the dog was chained outside without other facts is insufficient to impute knowledge to Ms. McDonald, particularly when she was the one who asked Mr. Fox to restrain the dog. She did so to appease the other tenant, not out of any fear of the dog's behavior. (*Orozco*)

Moreover, the mere existence of an article in the town paper reporting on a prior incident involving Mr. Fox's dog is insufficient to charge Ms. McDonald with constructive knowledge because an ordinarily prudent person would not scan local newspapers to check on whether a tenant's dog had acted viciously before. (*Georgianna*) Imposing that burden on a landlord would be both "oppressive and unreasonable." (*Georgianna*)

## Conclusion

Therefore, Ms. McDonald did not have the requisite knowledge.

# Chapter 7 Exercise Answer Key:

The answers on personal learning styles will vary from one student to another. There is no right answer. The purpose is for students to reflect on how they learn and then adapt their study habits to best fit their needs.

1. This answer will reveal whether the student is more of an auditory, visual or kinesthetic learner. Auditory learners like to work with sound and music whereas visual learners prefer images, pictures, and colors to organize information. Kinesthetic learners use their body and sense of touch to learn information.

2. This answer will help the student decide how to set up his or her study space. Among other things, the student should consider whether to sit at a desk or table or on the floor or not at all, whether the room should be dimly or brightly lit and quiet or loud, whether to work near other people (i.e. coffee house) or alone (in your room or office or a corner of the library), whether to listen to music, walk around, eat, drink or do something else at the same time or during a break, and the time when he or she works best (morning, afternoon, evening, etc.).

3. This answer will inform the student's decision on whether a study group would be a good fit for his or her needs.

4. The ground rules could describe logistical matters, such as where and for how long the group would meet, as well as substantive matters, such as what topics to cover and the method for doing so. Whatever ground rules the student decides, they need to be communicated to all group members at the beginning to ensure a collaborative and productive working relationship.

5. Some quick and fun activities include exercising, seeing a movie, reading a non-legal book, playing a game, and going out to dinner. The idea is that

the student should find time to take a short break from studying.  Time away from law school, even if brief, will help bring some balance into the student's life as well as energize that student to continue to work hard.

# Chapter 8 Exercise Answer Key:

This is a very reflective exercise.  Students tend to feel a mix of the emotions listed.  Also, they feel differently from one day to another.  The first semester of law school is usually when students feel most uncertain and anxious about their abilities.  If any of the negative feelings are so overwhelming that the student has trouble sleeping, eating, socializing, completing work on time or at all, or exhibits other signs of depression, the student should seek professional assistance from the law school administration or elsewhere immediately.  A student's health always takes priority over any assignment or other law school responsibility.

# INDEX

| | |
|---|---|
| Outlining: | The process of organizing your class notes, case briefs, and other materials from a course into a single document. A big part of the process is *Rule Synthesis*. The document will include all of the legal rules covered in a course and illustrate how those rules play out in various factual scenarios. The outline is invaluable in successfully preparing and studying for exams. |
| Persuasive Authority: | Authority that a court is not bound to follow. However, the court may be persuaded to look at that authority for guidance. For example, decisions by an inferior court are not binding on a higher court within a jurisdiction. Similarly, decisions by a court outside of a jurisdiction are not binding on a court within that jurisdiction, regardless of the levels of those courts. In both examples, those decisions would have a persuasive effect only. |
| Persuasive Writing: | Writing that argues that a certain outcome is the right one. This is usually the type of writing covered in second semester first-year writing courses where the main assignment is to write an appellate brief or trial brief or both. |
| Precedent: | Prior authority that establishes a rule or legal principle on the same or similar issue and facts as a problem you are analyzing. |
| Predictive Writing: | Writing that predicts the likely outcome of a legal problem. This is usually the type of writing covered in first semester first-year writing courses where the end project is to write an interoffice legal memorandum. |
| Rationale: | A court's reasoning or support for its decision. For example, the court might explain how case law, statutes, public policy, social justice, and legislative purpose or intent support its decision. That explanation is the court's rationale or reasoning. |
| Reasoning: | *See* explanation for Rationale |

| | |
|---|---|
| Reasoning By Analogy: | The process of explaining how a case is analogous to or distinguishable from precedent.  By reasoning by analogy to precedent, you can demonstrate that you applied the rule appropriately.  Your conclusion is thus reliable because it is consistent with the holdings in cases with like facts and distinct from the cases with distinguishable facts. |
| Relevant Facts: | These are legally significant facts.  The facts that the court relied on in reaching its decision or holding. |
| Rule: | The legal rule is a statement of the law that controls how an issue should be resolved. |
| Rule Application: | An illustration of how a legal rule is applied to a specific set of facts. |
| Rule Synthesis: | Developing a legal rule from the holdings of cases that address the same problem as yours. |
| Socratic Method: | A style of teaching, named after Socrates, the Athenian philosopher, who taught his students through questioning, not lecture, on the theory that they would discover the "truth" together.  Law professors who use this method typically will not lecture on the law.  Instead, they will teach the law by soliciting students' answers to a series of questions about the cases they assigned as well as by asking them to resolve hypothetical scenarios that address the same topic as the assigned cases but involve a slightly different set of circumstances. |
| Stare Decisis: | A short form of the Latin phrase *stare decisis et non quieta movere*.  It means "to stand by precedents and not to disturb settled principles of law."  According to this principle, judges should follow the rulings of prior decisions involving facts substantially similar to the ones before them.  The theory is that the law will be applied more consistently and fairly if judges abide by precedent. |

CPSIA information can be obtained
at www.ICGtesting.com
Printed in the USA
JSHW061015180723
44952JS00002B/201